"Take charge of your career path and get ahead with *Your Career Advantage*! Offering actionable steps you can start taking today, Caroline Dowd-Higgins empowers professionals to overcome obstacles and impact organizational culture to create the career and life they dream of."

— **Dr. Marshall Goldsmith, the Thinkers50 #1 Executive Coach and New York Times bestselling author of *The Earned Life*, *Triggers*, and *What Got You Here Won't Get You There***

"I've known Caroline Dowd-Higgins for a decade, and she is one of the top career strategists in the world. *Your Career Advantage* is a timely and compelling resource that offers you, the modern career professional, essential action steps to navigate challenges and showcase your successes to achieve the most rewarding career imaginable *without* sacrificing your all-important personal life."

— **James M. Citrin, Leader, Spencer Stuart CEO Practice, and bestselling author of *The Career Playbook* and *Leading at a Distance***

"She began her career as an opera singer, disrupted herself to become a corporate executive, and now she's a C-suite executive coach. If you want expert advice on how to reinvent yourself and gain an advantage in your career, read Caroline Dowd-Higgins' book. Clear, straightforward, highly practical."

— **Whitney Johnson, Thinkers50 Top 10 Management Thinker, *WSJ* and *USA Today* bestselling author of *Smart Growth***

"Caroline Dowd-Higgins, as always, blends pragmatic examples and advice with total relevance to meet the career challenges of today's leaders. Work is too crucial a part of our lives to remain unfulfilled or for us to resent the time and effort put in. This practical handbook offers sage insights and advice to create a better equilibrium, greater engagement, and commitment to being your best at work and in your personal life. This is about taking healthy and timely action. Remember, if you are not having fun, you are doing it wrong!"

— **Danielle Grant, MA, PCC, FHEA, FRSA, Director of LeaderShape Global Ltd, and coauthor of** *Leading Beyond the Ego* **and** *Transpersonal Leadership in Action*

"This insightful book offers essential action steps to help the modern career professional navigate challenges and showcase their successes to achieve a rewarding career without sacrificing their personal life."

— **Melissa Daimler, Chief Learning Officer, Udemy, and author of** *ReCulturing: Design Your Company Culture to Connect with Strategy and Purpose for Lasting Success*

"Balancing well-being and career advancement has become a serious challenge. Caroline Dowd-Higgins offers superb coaching insights to help professionals tackle this conundrum in ways that are satisfying, sustainable, and rewarding. Highly recommend!"

— **Sally Helgesen, Speaker and Leadership Coach, and author of** *How Women Rise, The Female Vision,* **and** *The Web of Inclusion*

"The world of work keeps changing, but *Your Career Advantage* offers professionals practical advice on how to future-proof their careers while building a rewarding work life now. Read this book to learn how to achieve success that feels good and helps others be their best, too."

— **Laura Vanderkam, author of** *Tranquility by Tuesday*

YOUR
CAREER
ADVANTAGE

*Overcome **Challenges** to
Achieve a **Rewarding** Work Life*

Sally,
Enjoy your career.
Love your life!
With gratitude,
Caroline Dowd-Higgins

YOUR CAREER ADVANTAGE

Overcome **Challenges** to Achieve a **Rewarding** Work Life

CAROLINE DOWD-HIGGINS

NICHE PRESSWORKS

Your Career Advantage: Overcome Challenges to Achieve a Rewarding Work Life
ISBN-13:   978-1-952654-64-0 Paperback
           978-1-952654-65-7 Hardback
           978-1-952654-66-4 eBook

Copyright © 2023 by Caroline Dowd-Higgins
All rights reserved. No part of this book may be used or reproduced in any manner whatsoever without prior written consent of the author, except as provided by the United States of America copyright law.
For permission to reprint portions of this content or bulk purchases, contact https://carolinedowdhiggins.com.

Published by Niche Pressworks; http://NichePressworks.com
Indianapolis, IN

The views expressed herein are solely those of the author and do not necessarily reflect the views of the publisher.

Author portrait by: Natalie Hugie, Noel Photos

DEDICATION

To David, for your unconditional love,
support, and encouragement.

PREFACE

My name is Caroline Dowd-Higgins. I am a speaker, author, executive coach, and host of the global podcast, *Your Working Life.* I have held executive leadership roles in several organizations, and I continue to be on the front lines of the future-focused workplace experience in my consulting practice. I have engaged with leaders, influencers, authors, and researchers from around the world who have shared their savvy insights about how to navigate the world of work successfully — and I am a recovering workaholic.

I didn't fully understand it until recently, but over many years, I had become addicted to work. Addiction is characterized by an intense urge to engage in certain behaviors — in my case, a compulsive engagement to work. The perpetual work had short-term rewards like the euphoric dopamine hit of recognition, money, and advancement, but the long-term costs were debilitating to my health and detrimental to my personal life.

I was working so much that I was missing my life, and I was enabled by a global culture that celebrates and encourages overworking. My work treadmill speed was set so fast that getting off seemed more dangerous than hanging on and keeping up.

I was celebrated for being a workhorse, accomplishing difficult things, and rising to any challenge without question. I was in denial that I was not fully present with family and friends and regularly turned down opportunities to do nonwork-related activities, which created a vicious cycle of work-sleep-repeat. Even vacations became other places to do my work. I felt like I was living a recurring Groundhog's Day, and it began to compromise my well-being.

Then, I hit a wall.

One evening, I was working well past a normal quitting time when I noticed painful red welts on my legs and torso. Since it was after-hours for my doctor, I consulted the Internet for answers, and I learned that the hives were most likely brought on by stress. My doctor confirmed this and explained that it was a clear warning sign that I needed to recalibrate and take stock of my health. The hives were evidence that something needed to change, or more serious health issues could follow. This was my wake-up call and the catalyst for a drastic change.

Choices and Changes

Nobody forced me into my work addiction. While many industries and organizations actively seek individuals with the compulsion-to-work trait and then exploit this behavior to their benefit, I alone had the power to recognize and reprogram my behavior. You always have choices.

One of my first big career changes happened when I transitioned from the world of professional opera to the business and higher-education arenas, where I worked for two decades.

I loved my career as an opera singer until it stopped loving me. Consistent work was difficult to find, and the starving artist's feast-or-famine existence was not enjoyable or sustainable.

My first book, *This Is Not the Career I Ordered: Empowering Strategies from Women Who Recharged, Reignited, and Reinvented Their Careers*, chronicles my career reinvention from the music world to the business world and the process I went through to find a new path. I showcase stories of several women who made career changes and share action steps for discovering your values and strengths to start anew.

While I made many career choices in the business world, my next big change came when I made the bold decision to end my codependency working as an employee for an organization and chose to go out on my own. I took my side hustle in executive coaching, speaking, and consulting full-time. I mustered the courage to make a shift that empowered me to have a vibrant career and a fulfilling personal life.

As an executive coach, I have helped hundreds of clients find their best work/life integration to manage a career and personal life together. Yet, my own life was not reflective of how I was coaching others until I made another choice — probably the hardest choice yet.

I acknowledged my work addiction and recognized that it was not in alignment with what I knew to be true or how I was coaching my clients. More importantly, it did not reflect my values and did not reflect what I wanted out of life. I made a conscious choice to change. I embraced my fear and started the hard work of unlearning unhealthy behaviors and developing new work and life habits.

Like many, the post-pandemic experience also inspired deep self-reflection and pushed me to consider what was important as I started to navigate my life and career moving forward. That experience was the genesis of this book.

The modern careerist is facing unique challenges, like remote, hybrid, or required on-location work that impacts life and career. Some organizations are struggling with the concept of flexible work, and others are embracing customized schedules, unlimited vacation time, and other innovative practices to create workplace cultures that promote well-being and happiness to retain top talent. People are the most valuable asset in every organization, and companies must think again about how to design a workplace where individuals can do their best work.

I wrote this book to address issues impacting future-focused professionals (think midcareer professionals seeking advancement, first-time C-suite leaders, pinnacle leaders, etc.) and to provide solutions and action steps to help them —and you — thrive.

You are in the trenches — leading people, tackling complex scenarios, and artfully setting strategies to empower your organizations to be competitive and successful. Perhaps you are struggling with work addiction tendencies. This book is a resource to help you honor your career aspirations and overcome obstacles so you can be the best version of yourself and model positive behaviors for others.

As an executive coach, I hear the good, the bad, and the ugly from clients dealing with difficult bosses, dead-end roles, or toxic work environments that promote workaholism. I also have clients who work in enlightened organizations that honor people and celebrate great work to create an authentic sense of belonging for colleagues. I've held executive leadership roles in several organizations and lived these experiences myself. I sought the insight of coaches, trusted sponsors, and mentors to help me make sense of difficult scenarios, celebrate my successes, and strategize for my career advancement.

What I know for sure is that you are more in control of your career and life success, happiness, and satisfaction than you might think. Smart and savvy professionals seek help — it's a strength and not a sign of weakness. I will help by sharing what is rarely talked about in the workplace (but should be!) and empower you with solutions to help you prosper. You will learn to recognize and mitigate your blind spots to forge a path that is self-actualized and fulfilling.

It's tough out there, and you don't need to walk your career path alone. Think of me as your personal executive coach. I am always at-the-ready to help you find *Your Career Advantage*, so you can overcome challenges and honor your accomplishments to achieve a rewarding work life now.

TABLE OF CONTENTS

MOVING UP OR MOVING ON
Should I Stay, or Should I Go?   7

THRIVE WHERE YOU ARE
Leverage Opportunity Where You Are Now   49

CHALLENGES THAT SUCK
Let's Get Real; Shit Happens   87

ENJOY YOUR CAREER AND LOVE YOUR LIFE

Your career directly impacts your quality of life. Full stop. In this book, I will show you how to maximize your career fulfillment so you can also love your life. It need not be an either/or scenario — you deserve to honor your career **and** your life at the same time.

I use my own real-life experiences as well as stories from colleagues and clients to demonstrate how these topics can impact the world of work. Our experiences come from organizations of all sizes, so the lessons apply to a myriad of scenarios. Colleagues' and clients' names have been changed to honor their anonymity.

Navigating career advancement and honing leadership skills can be challenging to figure out on your own, so let's get started.

How to Use This Book

This book is organized into six sections — each reflecting an important topic currently challenging many in the world of work. These six topics are by far the most requested issues I work on with both my executive coaching clients and organizations in my consulting practice. They are relevant to every industry, and I believe they will be relatable to you. Let me give you an overview of what to expect.

1. **Moving Up or Moving On: Should I stay, or should I go?**
   Talent wars are in full swing, and professionals have options about where they work and how to advance their careers. The grass is not always greener in another organization, but you need not suffer in a bad situation, for instance, with a hellish boss. This section will help you navigate career advancement and learn how to identify the leaders with whom you want to work.

2. **Thrive Where You Are: Leveraging opportunity where you are now.**
   If you like your organization and need only a few tweaks to refresh and renew your engagement and gain greater satisfaction, then this section will help you flourish. From productivity hacks to finding what you love in your work, this section will help you discover how to reinvigorate your career in the organization where you work now.

3. **Challenges That Suck: Let's get real; shit happens.**
   Dysfunctional work relationships are real. Navigating the good, the bad, and the ugly of workplace relationships

can be exhausting. This section dives into what's really happening at work that nobody wants to talk about (but should!). It provides you with actionable tactics to hone your grit and clear away the crap to make room for solutions you can live with.

4. **Well-Being at Work: How to excel in your career and honor your health.**
   Depression, anxiety, and exhaustion are at an all-time high around the world. It's time to get real about how you can live a healthy life at work and at home. The goal is to develop skills so you can excel in your career and live a positive, healthy life. This section provides practical and implementable insight to honor the only body you have.

5. **The Office Vibe: Company culture matters.**
   Ping-pong tables and fancy coffee bars do not make company culture. It's time to focus on what corporate culture really means and learn how to design, live, and breathe a culture that comes from the people who work in the organization. This section will help you design a place where you can do your best work.

6. **Future-Proof Your Career: Sought-after leaders continue to develop.**
   The world of work has irrevocably changed, and savvy leaders need to embrace and hone their emotional intelligence to advance their careers and recruit and retain top talent in their organizations with a future-focused mindset. This section reveals what the future of work looks like and how you can create your distinct advantage.

Actionable Insights

Each section contains a series of short, pithy chapters filled with relatable challenges, real-life stories, and resourceful solutions. You can read the book from beginning to end to get the full executive coaching experience but also keep it handy as a resource. Use it to help you when a particular challenge surfaces and you need advice in real time.

At the end of each chapter, you will find a **Pro Tips** section that lists the chapter's salient ideas as well as actionable steps. You can also use the Pro Tips as sharable sound bites. I encourage you to share them on your favorite social media platforms and with colleagues, direct reports, or friends who need a helping hand. Use the **#YourCareerAdvantage** hashtag to become part of the *Your Career Advantage* community. Pro Tips are a great way to pay it forward and help another in need.

Let's Get Started!

Your Career Advantage will help you future-proof your career. You'll learn how to handle volatile, uncertain, complex, and ambiguous (VUCA) work environments where you will not simply survive but flourish.

Along the way, I will help you identify the qualities and skills that will make you the best version of yourself. This self-knowledge will prepare you to pursue careers in organizations or entrepreneurial ventures where you can achieve the goals you set and do your best work. You will be empowered to gain new perspectives, prepared to handle challenges directly, and pushed to up your game. The goal? To live the life you want to lead as you excel in your career.

Often, all it takes is a small tweak or reframe to turn a challenge into an opportunity. There are indeed moments when work sucks, but suffering is optional. It's time to own the power you already have to activate your best self.

I am dedicated to helping you live a vibrant life and an accomplished career — today. It starts with *Your Career Advantage*!

MOVING UP
OR MOVING ON

Should I Stay, or Should I Go?

CHAPTER 1

GO AHEAD,
BE AMBITIOUS!

The career landscape provides you with a myriad of choices about where to work and how to advance your career. This section will help you become a promotable player and confidently consider the leaders with whom you want to work — or not.

During a mock interview with my client Collette, I asked her if she considered herself ambitious, and she recoiled as if I had used an inappropriate word. Keep in mind, Collette is a focused, smart, and confident woman pursuing her first senior executive leadership role. But this question struck a nerve. She revealed that she never wanted to be seen as the run-over-your-colleague type of ambitious person, and she thought being ambitious would jeopardize her professional brand and good coworker persona.

This led to an interesting discussion about good and bad ambitious behaviors. While we agreed that some ambitious behaviors are negative (i.e., being pushy, ruthless, power-hungry), Collette was surprised by the positive aspects of ambition. She hadn't considered how ambition could motivate and encourage her to engage with her work in more meaningful ways. We created a list of definitions for positive ambition, including go-getter, determined, and motivated. This reframing of ambition resonated with Collette, and she now owns it as part of her brand narrative.

How Ambitious Should You Be?

Your definition of ambition is yours to design, so give yourself permission to reframe it as part of your *professional aspiration*. As you consider what ambition means to you, reflect on the following to help organize your thoughts:

- Define who you are on your own terms.
- Be clear about how you want others in the career world to perceive you.
- Make an effort to put that out into the world.

Focus on how ambition positively showcases your motivation and eagerness to advance. It gives you the ability to handle change and tackle new challenges with an "I'm ready for the opportunity" mindset. Then, put it into action. If your boss asks about your career goals, be prepared with an answer and ready to aim high if that reflects your intentions.

I worked with Collette to help her articulate her goals clearly and then communicate those goals with her network and in interviews so others understood exactly what she aspired to do.

There is no mind reading in the career world, and this clarity and conviction helped Collette land the role she sought.

Aiming low and acting too humbly will inhibit your career growth because others will not believe you are interested in new challenges. If you are ambitious, as I am, wear it with pride and own your self-confidence by talking about what you want and how you will go about earning it.

Ambition Action Plan

Once you've defined what ambition means to you, access that power to make an action plan that will motivate you to engage with your work in more meaningful ways.

1. **Set goals.** Set actionable goals for yourself and find accountability partners to keep you on track.

2. **Take risks.** Ambitious people are not afraid to take risks and make mistakes. Failing forward is an investment in your growth and illustrates your ability to be resilient.

3. **Invest in yourself.** You are your most valuable investment. Investing in yourself isn't just about spending your money. Take time for yourself. Make yourself a priority, and others will see you as such.

4. **Eliminate negativity.** Negativity is debilitating — from both the outside world and from within. Negativity only holds you back; it keeps you from seeing the positive and the prospects on the horizon. Don't tear yourself or your

work apart. Don't compare yourself to others. Work on yourself, your goals, and what you want to accomplish. Keep that end in sight. Your biggest competition is yourself and no one else. Strive to be better than you were yesterday and focus on your personal best.

5. **Don't wait.** If you keep waiting, you'll never accomplish your goals. If you keep saying tomorrow, tomorrow will never come. Why not start now? You can't expect great things to happen when you've done little or nothing to work for them. Push yourself, fight for what you want, and don't take no for an answer. You must make things happen, or your career and life will happen by default.

6. **Surround yourself with healthy, ambitious people.** Surround yourself with people who will lift you up, people who will push you as they push themselves, and people who know what they want and are willing to fight for it. If you want to keep working toward your goals, you need people around you who are doing the same. Start spending time with other ambitious people, and you will energize each other.

Celebrate Your Ambition

By putting your professional goals out into the world, you are more likely to create opportunities that align with your values because others will have a clear expectation of what you want. Take pride in your ambition and own it with a confidence that is professionally palatable and will position you to be considered for new opportunities you seek.

PRO TIPS

- Focus on what you aspire to do and show the world that you are ready for a new opportunity.

- Create an action plan — set goals, take risks, and invest in yourself.

- Concentrate on what you are doing that's positive and surround yourself with people who ignite your energy to move forward.

- Set daily goals to keep yourself moving forward, avoiding the status quo trap.

- Be specific when sharing your ambition with others, so they can help you move forward.

CHAPTER 2

ADVANCE YOUR CAREER WITH A SPONSOR

If you feel like your career has plateaued or that you're being overlooked for opportunities, it's time to take charge of your professional future.

In many cases, your boss is too busy doing their own work to spend time pondering how they can help you grow or promote you. Especially if you're a high performer, you may be left alone because you don't cause trouble and don't need much help.

In today's world of work, just doing great work isn't enough. You need to define your distinguishing strengths and value-add so you can be seen, heard, and considered for the new opportunities you seek. It's time to get in the driver's seat and be strategic about how you navigate new opportunities. The fastest way to get all of this done is to find a sponsor.

Mentors vs. Sponsors

Both mentors and sponsors are an enormous help to your career, but they serve different purposes. Mentors provide you with wisdom and encouragement. They are incredibly helpful and work with you to resolve and learn from challenges. I strongly encourage you to seek out mentors and to be a mentor to others.

Sponsors, on the other hand, serve as career advocates on a higher level. They put their professional reputation on the line to advocate for your advancement. Sponsors use their power and influence on your behalf. Sponsorship is how power is transferred in the workplace.

You can't ask for a sponsor. Typically, they find you. How does that happen? It's easy. You do great work and get recognized by someone who sees your potential. Sponsors seek you out because of your results-oriented work, attitude, and professional value.

Identifying Potential Sponsors

While you can't ask for a sponsor, you can identify influencers. Who do you admire and seek to emulate based on their achievements or behavior in the career world? Consider people you know as well as those you aspire to know. Generate a list of names.

Before you begin meeting with influencers, you need to be clear about what you have to offer and what you seek. It's time to define what makes you unique and valuable. Consider the narrative you want to share. Keep it succinct and compelling. This is the story an influencer may use to describe you when you are not present.

Next, be clear about your future goals and/or areas of interest. Specificity is key. If an influencer becomes a sponsor, they want to know exactly how they can help you. If you are uncertain about future goals, spend time with an executive coach or someone you trust to identify what you want and get the support you need to move forward.

Push Your Limits

A sponsor may consider you for a role or organization that is very different from where your career is now. Be open to change and new possibilities since growth requires stepping away from your comfort zone. I will tell you from personal experience, I have benefitted from sponsors who recruited me for roles I would not have considered if it were not for their advocacy. They pushed me to try different things and develop skills and strengths I wasn't currently showcasing.

I am forever grateful that they encouraged me and had faith in me. It's time to stop letting fear control your willingness to take a risk and try something new. Know that you can always fail forward and learn from every experience. You won't achieve your full potential if you always play it safe, so expand your comfort zone and challenge yourself with something different.

Virtuous Circle of Support

In addition to a sponsor, I also like to have what I call my personal board of directors. This group of individuals helps me navigate my life and career. When creating this group, think about what you need and seek individuals who have specific wisdom to share. Earn the right to ask for their support by showcasing your great work and always reciprocate by asking, "How can I help you?"

I find my board of directors by cultivating relationships in my network with individuals who have abilities I admire and can learn from. Most importantly, these individuals have seen me in action and have a clear sense of my work and expertise. Here are some cast members to consider for your personal board of directors.

1. **Mentor** – Provides advice, support, or feedback.

2. **Strategic Thinker** – Helps strategize an action plan to get ahead.

3. **Connector** – Makes introductions to influential people and talks you up with their peers.

4. **Opportunity Giver** – Provides high-visibility support.

5. **Advocate** – Publicly advocates and fights for you in settings where you can't fight for yourself.

Toot Your Own Professional Horn

The ideal professional persona projects ability without attitude since nobody appreciates a bragger who has gone to the dark side of obnoxiousness. However, humility won't land you the job or the promotion, so you must talk about the accomplishments you have earned with confidence.

Be ready to talk about your strengths and accomplishments and not just during the interview or the performance evaluation. Have your stories at the ready to illustrate your skills with specific examples so it feels conversational. Own what you have achieved and accept the credit you deserve. You must learn to be your own best self-advocate and speak articulately about your accomplishments — especially with sponsors who can help you move forward.

Pay It Forward

I am grateful to the many mentors, influencers, sponsors, connectors, strategic thinkers, and advocates who have helped me forge my career path. I take great responsibility when helping others, as I have been helped, to keep the virtuous circle of support ongoing. Consider who in your network needs support and how you might lend a helping hand.

Enhance Your Elevation Opportunities

There's no secret formula for career advancement. It's a combination of your expertise and relationships. With these tools, you position yourself for success and have the potential to elevate your career.

Circulate with people who challenge, stimulate, and inspire you to do your very best, and be clear about what you want and what you have to offer. Spending time with high-achieving, promotable players who bring out your best qualities will help you get noticed. These actions can position you to attract a sponsor and elevate your opportunities.

PRO TIPS

- Be clear about what you have to offer and what you seek so others can advocate for you when you are not present.

- Identify influencers whom you admire based on their achievements or behavior in the career world.

- Develop your personal board of directors with individuals who can help you navigate advancement.

- Be open to change and new possibilities since growth requires stepping away from your comfort zone.

CHAPTER 3

WHO'S GOT YOUR BACK?

One-and-done connections leave people feeling ill-used. Networking is an important skill, and it takes diligence and intentionality to maintain the extended community you've worked so hard to develop. The secret to maintaining strong professional relationships? Follow-up.

When you authentically nurture and steward your network, you develop deeper relationships — people who will stick with you through thick and thin. If you are lucky, you will sustain some lifelong relationships with individuals who will always have your back.

Bryan's Microsoft Adventure

My client Bryan has always wanted to work at Microsoft. He followed media stories featuring Microsoft leaders, kept apprised of new products and tech solutions, and applied regularly to posted roles (with nary a response). Then, while attending a national tech conference, he fortuitously found himself seated next to a Microsoft employee named Mindy. The two struck up the typical conference conversation, exchanging brief pleasantries and business cards, and Bryan followed up with her a week after the conference ended.

He shared an article he thought his new Microsoft friend, Mindy, would appreciate and asked for a brief call to learn more about her role and the company culture of the iconic tech firm. Over the next six months, a rapport grew between the two, and Bryan kept checking in every few weeks with salient articles, videos, and brief notes to keep his new professional acquaintance in the know. He also asked how he could help her. It turned out that Mindy's son was interested in attending New York University, where Bryan had earned his MBA. Bryan spoke to Mindy's son about his experience at NYU and provided a safe space for him to ask questions.

Bryan and Mindy kept in touch for over a year. When Bryan's dream role at Microsoft became available, Mindy introduced him to the hiring manager in the department, and his resume rose to the top of the pile. While he did not land that role, the hiring manager was impressed with Bryan and the recommendation from Mindy. He offered him a different role at Microsoft.

Bryan's story is a testimony to the power of authentic relationship-building and nurturing. He understood that networking worked in both directions and looked for ways to help Mindy. Making this effort keeps the relationship equitable. Bryan loves working at Microsoft, and now he has Mindy as a colleague. They continue to have each other's backs.

Nurture Your Network

Commit to keeping strong relationships with the people in your network who matter and make time to nurture those connections. Schedule reminders in your calendar to make certain you reach out to these individuals on a regular basis. Even a brief note can keep the connection strong.

In a sensory world, I sometimes like to call my connections — instead of sending an email or text. It's refreshing to call simply to touch base instead of always making an ask. No need to have an agenda or a reason.

Another personal favorite is sending a handwritten note. Written correspondence is a dying art, so you can distinguish yourself with this technique. A brief note of thanks, encouragement, or just saying hello is an opportunity to nurture a relationship.

Be Curious and Help

Reaching out to connections can easily fall to the bottom of a busy to-do list, but it's important and works best with consistency. Decide how often you'd like to communicate with your network and add reminders to your calendar to reach out. Use these touchpoints to focus on how you can help the other person, and don't focus on what you need.

If you aren't sure what to say or do, here are three options.

- **Interests** – Learn about your connections' interests by asking what they are interested in. Then, send related resources like articles, TED Talks, podcasts, etc. You don't have to share the same interests to be on the lookout for something they may find useful. It doesn't have to be professional — finding information about your colleague's vintage jewelry collection is a great way to touch base and show that you care.

- **Goals** – Learn about their goals. When you know what other people are working to achieve, you are in a better position to assist. Ask them what they need, then listen and look for ways to help.

- **Help** – Offer to help and then help. Be a connector, share ideas and information, and offer to help when you can. Be sure to follow up and keep your promises because the connector relationship can be very powerful. Even better, consider how you can help with a random act of kindness that is unexpected.

Follow-Up Is Critical

Be consistent about following up on all commitments you make. Period. Consider the time frame and cadence of how you communicate with your network. Don't let too much time pass before you reach out, or the relationship will gather dust.

Keep your focus on helping, aiding, and assisting the other person, and don't focus on what you need. The seeds you plant by assisting another will grow into great things for you.

Start now and commit to nurturing your network on a regular basis. If your contact list is large, then do this incrementally and systematically so the task is enjoyable and feasible.

PRO TIPS

- Commit to keeping the relationships that matter and nurture your network.

- Call or send a handwritten note to break through the digital overwhelm of emails and texts.

- Be curious and learn about another's goals and interests.

- Offer to help and be true to your word.

- Follow-up is critical, especially with a new relationship you want to cultivate.

- Keep your focus on helping, aiding, and assisting the other person, and don't focus on what you need.

CHAPTER 4

A CAREER TRAJECTORY WITH SMART GROWTH

As an executive coach, I have long believed you need to be at the ready with a professional exit and/or growth strategy, even if you are blissfully happy in a current role. Change is constant, and there is tremendous growth in the workplace, which is a ripe opportunity for advancement or transition.

As a guest on my *Your Working Life* podcast, Whitney Johnson cracked open this important conversation around growth and how we experience it. Her book, *Smart Growth: How to Grow Your People to Grow Your Company*, provides a model to help people think about where they are and what's next, and she shares wisdom about helping people develop to their full potential.[1]

The S Curve of Learning

Johnson uses a simple visual model to demystify the process of growth. Called the S Curve of Learning, it illustrates how every new skill learned and every challenge faced takes the form of a distinct learning curve. The S Curve of Learning can help leaders grow their organizations, attract and retain top talent, execute succession planning, and configure a team. Johnson posits that people aren't the most valuable resource of an organization — they *are* the organization.

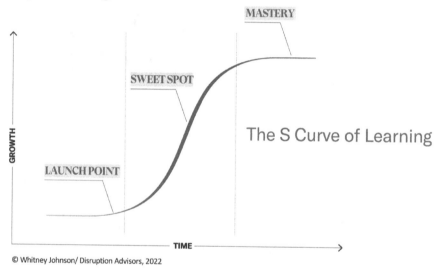

© Whitney Johnson/ Disruption Advisors, 2022

Growth on the S Curve

Johnson's S Curve tracks an individual's growth from the very beginning (when learning new skills) to mastery. Organizations can use this knowledge to help develop talent by identifying which phase employees are in and using that information to support and encourage their development.

Johnson organizes the growth and learning journey along the S Curve into three phases:

Launch Point

- Individuals at this stage are generally new to a role, encountering new challenges and often needing additional support.
- Their new perspective, or fresh eyes, can offer valuable insights.
- Growth feels slow at this stage.

Sweet Spot

- Individuals here enjoy the challenge and effectively putting their experience and information to work.
- Work remains challenging but also more familiar — hard, but not too hard, and easy, but not too easy.
- Momentum happens with focus, and growth is fast.

Mastery

- Individuals at this stage have accomplished what they set out to do.
- Work that once was challenging has become easy, and growth slows. People may become bored.
- Growth at this point comes either from big challenges in a current role or from a transition to a new role in (or out of) the organization.

As individuals grow and learn, so, too, do organizations and communities. Growth is learning put into action —

action that betters the world as we better ourselves and our small niches, both personal and professional. Johnson shares that growth occurs when learning is internalized — when we try something new and invest the effort to move it from being something we do to something we are.

A Portfolio of Learning Curves

Leaders must be aware of the stages of each direct report's S Curve and help them become accountable for their own growth and development.

At the launch point, people are often thrown into challenging jobs that they're not completely prepared for, and leaders need to make sure they have access to a great support team. At the other end of the curve, it's important to recognize the risks of keeping people who've reached the mastery stage in a role for too long. An employee can become complacent or a flight risk.

If growth is nurtured along the entire S Curve, change develops naturally. Succession plans across the organization become clearer, and internal talent can be optimized to develop a deep bench that honors all levels in the organization — the entry level, the sweet spot crew in the middle, and the seasoned leaders.

When Should You Grow?

It's important to be keenly self-aware of where you are and where you want to be. As a team leader, it's equally important to be aware of where your people are and how you can help them reach their greatest potential.

When thinking of a growth trajectory, you need to consider both long- and short-term goals. This can be challenging, but Johnson has created a list of seven steps that will help individuals and team leaders learn and grow careers. She calls these the **Seven Accelerants for the Future,** as follows:

1. **Identify the right risks.** What risks could you take in your current role? Can you play where others aren't?

2. **Play to your distinctive strengths.** What do others see as your strengths? How can you better leverage them in your current (or future) role?

3. **Embrace constraints.** How can you use time/resource constraints to help you stretch your personal growth and become more innovative?

4. **Challenge entitlement.** Who do you need to listen to that you don't now? How can you avoid "them and us" thinking and/or believing that you are always right?

5. **Step back and grow.** What do you need to let go of to grow? Attitude, reliance on something or someone, etc.?

6. **Failure is learning**. What failures should you acknowledge? How did you fail forward, and what did you learn?

7. **Be discovery driven.** What is your learning goal for the next few weeks? Once you achieve a goal, take a moment to reflect, adapt, and consider what is next.

Action Steps

The post-pandemic journey has, out of necessity, sharpened our ability to deal with ambiguity and change. Savvy leaders must be mindful of the virtuous (not vicious) growth cycle and invest in the growth and development of their people for the good of the individuals and the success of the organization.

As you navigate your own career growth, take time to evaluate where you are on the S Curve of Learning, and consider where you want to be. Professional growth and development are the combined responsibility of leadership and the individual. Reflect on whether you are a promotable player and what you need to do to design a career future that honors you.

PRO TIPS

- Always be ready with a professional exit and/or a growth strategy, even if you are happy in your current role.

- Establish where you are on the S Curve of Learning: Launch Point, Sweet Spot, or Mastery.

- Focus on the Seven Accelerants for the Future to disrupt your status quo and grow:

  - Identify the risks
  - Play to your strengths
  - Embrace constraints
  - Challenge entitlement
  - Step back and grow
  - Failure is learning
  - Be discovery driven

CHAPTER 5

THIS IS NOT THE BOSS I ORDERED

The current job market favors workers, which gives professionals the opportunity to reconsider their values and assess whether their current workplace is the best fit. As an executive coach, I'm regularly asked by clients, "Should I stay, or should I go?" as they contemplate where they can do their best work.

Leaders impact the organizational culture, success, vision, and productivity of the company workforce. Your boss has a pivotal role in decisions that are made about you when you are not in the room to self-advocate. Determining where you can do your best work has a lot to do with the leader to whom you report.

My Boss Sucks

There's an adage that still rings true: People don't quit organizations; they quit bad bosses. Not every leader is well suited for leadership-level responsibilities, which require a strong commitment to developing others. While bad bosses are a fact of life, we must also acknowledge that finding the unicorn-best boss is also unrealistic and may never happen. What's most important when making a stay-or-go decision is recognizing that the crummy boss you have now may not be there for the long haul. You need to factor in how you feel about the entire organization.

If you decide it's time to change and you're seeking new opportunities, it's essential to interview prospective bosses before accepting a new role. I'll share details on how to do that in the next chapter. For now, let's consider what to do if you like your work mission and your organization, but your boss sucks.

Mary Abbajay's book, *Managing Up: How to Move Up, Win at Work, and Succeed with Any Type of Boss,* helps you become a boss detective so you can piece together and solve the puzzle that is your boss. [2]

Boss Assessment 101

According to Abbajay, you need to learn how your boss ticks by identifying who works well with them and why. Listen carefully and notice patterns of behavior so you can learn to communicate in a way that resonates with their style.

Ask yourself the following questions:

- What is your boss's work-style personality? How do they interact with others?
- How does your boss like to receive information? How do they communicate?
- What are your boss's priorities? What are their goals? What are their concerns, challenges, and pressures?
- What is their boss like, and what does the organization expect from them?
- What does your boss expect from you?
- What are their pet peeves, and what truly matters to them?

The list could be endless. From my coaching vantage point, many people experience conflict with colleagues and bosses at work because they have not taken the time to understand each other and establish the two-way rules of engagement.

Is the Grass Really Greener Elsewhere?

Let me be clear: If you are experiencing egregious behavior from your boss, like harassment, misconduct, or unethical practices, then, by all means, get out fast.

But if you are on the fence about whether to stay or move on, here are a few more questions to consider before you decide.

- Do you love the work tasks and the mission of the organization? Does this position play to your strengths?
- Do you need the job financially or for benefits, like healthcare and a 401K?
- Are this role and the organization enhancing your future career development and upward mobility?

- Where are you on a scale from happy to stressed?
- Where is your boss on the scale of difficulty?
- What are the politics and organizational culture of the company?
- Do you want to survive or thrive?

 Clarity on Workplace Values

Studies of multigenerational workers indicate a common thread in desired workplace values:

- Good work/life integration
- Learning and development opportunities
- High salary or other financial benefits
- Positive workplace culture
- Opportunities for career advancement
- Sense of meaning at work
- Flexible work model

We have five generations in the workforce today, and the consensus is that workplace values matter and impact where people choose to work.

Sunday Night Blues

How do you really know if you are ready to move on or if you should buck up and stick it out? My belief has always been, "The suckiness is real, but the suffering is optional." As I explained in my TEDxWomen talk, you need to reframe failure and define success on your own terms. To make an informed decision, you must get quiet with yourself and reflect on how your work is impacting your life and career.[3]

A good gauge of how things are going can be measured by whether or not you're experiencing the Sunday Night Blues — an anxious feeling that starts on Sunday at about 5:00 p.m. when people realize the work week starts tomorrow. If you get this gnawing feeling every Sunday night, it's time to assess your work situation. Consider the following questions to help you decide your next steps.

- Are you unhappy most of every day doing this work?
- Is the work environment tainted with extreme toxicity, including your boss and your colleagues?
- Are the skills you've been hired to use for this job not things you're good at or enjoy?
- Do you believe, deep down, that you're meant for better, bigger, and more meaningful things?
- Do the outcomes you're working toward feel meaningless or negative to you?

You must seek no-nonsense clarity about your current career scenario before you consider your next move, and that's a lot to consider. Real-life gravity problems, like healthcare benefits, a secure salary that covers your debt, or a tuition reimbursement program, may be keeping you in a role for now. Changes that are beyond your control can also happen — like mergers, acquisitions, recessions, downsizing, and layoffs.

Ultimately, it is incumbent upon you to be ready for what's next by nurturing your network. You need to be seen and heard for your good work beyond your organization. Be known as a recruitable player and future-proof your career.

You Deserve a Place Where You Can Do Your Best Work

While a hot job market favors talented professionals, it's never wise to run away quickly from a bad role or a bad boss unless the situation is harmful or unethical. Before making any big changes, flip your perspective and focus on running toward something you are truly excited about that plays to your strengths and allows you to continue to grow.

When considering a new role many years ago, a wise mentor told me to always ask myself, "Is this a place where I can do my best work?" That has been my north star in career decision-making, and I believe it will help you moving forward.

PRO TIPS

- Reflect on your current work scenario and ask the tough questions to determine if your boss and your company honor your work values.

- Ascertain whether the role and your boss are allowing you to play to your strengths while also providing growth and professional development opportunities.

- Consider your gravity problems (benefits, salary, etc.) and determine if they could be solved with a career move.

- Decide whether you can improve the situation with your boss by setting clear expectations and communicating ground rules.

- Run toward something exciting that honors what you need instead of running away from something that you don't like.

CHAPTER **6**

INTERVIEW YOUR PROSPECTIVE BOSS

I f you are looking for a new career opportunity, don't miss out on the chance to interview your prospective boss to determine if they are the best fit for you. Your success and satisfaction are aligned with the leadership to whom you report, so remember that you are interviewing your future boss as much as they are interviewing you.

Over the last decade, I've practiced what I preach in this realm and have interviewed prospective bosses before accepting any new roles. These conversations set me up for success and opened my eyes to the types of leaders I wanted to work alongside.

Culture Clues

Depending on the role and the organization, you may not even set eyes on your prospective boss until you are a finalist for the role you seek. Keep your eyes and ears open during the hiring process to sleuth out company culture and evaluate how people treat each other. Are they smiling during the interview, even on Zoom? Do they look and act enthusiastic and engaged? How are they treating each other as colleagues?

If an onsite interview is part of the experience, look around and see how people are behaving. What's the mood of the team? Is it a sea of headphone-clad professionals in cubicles, or are people engaging with each other? These are clues that will help you decide if this is an environment where you can do your best work.

The Interview Ask

You know that it's imperative to come to every interview with questions for the team. Interviewing a potential boss requires a separate and private conversation. When you become a finalist, it's time to ask the hiring manager to schedule a separate, 30-minute conversation with you and your prospective boss. Explain that this is your opportunity to get to know the leader better and to determine if the hire is a mutually beneficial fit. A one-on-one conversation will allow you to get to know each other. Avoid a lunch meeting since it can be distracting and does not allow for a private and focused conversation.

I encourage you (as the candidate) to take copious notes during this conversation. This allows you to factor the answers into your decision-making process if you are ultimately extended an offer. If you are in consideration for a C-suite role, you should also plan to meet with the other C-level executives and members of the board to determine your best fit.

Interview Questions for Your Boss-to-Be

Remember, the spirit of the conversation with your boss-to-be is to learn more about them. You want to learn if you are simpatico by discussing what you value in a leader and work environment. Keep the meeting conversational and honor the 30-minute meeting request. If they extend the conversation, this is bonus time with your prospective boss and a very good sign.

Here is a list of my favorite questions. Feel free to customize for your specific needs or add your own. Only you can decide which questions are most relevant to you.

1. How do you prefer to communicate?
2. What's the best way to ask for your input and feedback?
3. How do you give constructive feedback? Do you welcome it from others?
4. What are the biggest strengths and challenges of the team?
5. What can I do to support the team and add value to the organization?
6. What would you add or subtract from your current team to strengthen performance or productivity?
7. With whom should I meet outside of the team to learn more about this role?
8. I value a culture with psychological safety. (Defined as a team or organizational climate characterized by interpersonal trust and a climate of respect. Individuals feel free to collaborate and feel safe taking risks or making mistakes, which ultimately enables the team to implement rapid innovation.) Does psychological safety exist on this team?

9. What aspect of the team/company culture do you wish to develop and nurture?

10. Do I have your permission to take innovative risks, fail forward, and showcase resilience when things don't work out?

11. What does success look like to you?

12. What is a misconception people have about you, and why?

13. How do you prepare and develop direct reports for advancement?

14. How do you recharge and tend to your self-care?

15. What else do I need to know about you that I have not asked?

Decision Time

After you interview your prospective boss, you must take the time to reflect on whether they are a good fit for your work style and your future career goals. We spend many waking hours at work, and our relationship with our direct leader impacts our personal and professional satisfaction, productivity, and advancement.

Be a bold and savvy candidate; ask your future boss for a brief conversation, so you can interview them and determine if this is a professional match you want to pursue. I know from experience that it's 30 minutes well spent.

PRO TIPS

- When you become a final-round candidate, schedule a 30-minute interview with your prospective boss to determine if they are a good fit for you.

- An interview is as much about you interviewing your prospective boss and colleagues as it is about them interviewing you.

- The spirit of the conversation with your boss-to-be is to learn more about them and to find out if you are simpatico.

- Refer to the sample questions in the chapter and add your own to learn what's important to you as you make the decision about accepting the role or not.

- Reflect on whether they are a good fit for your work style and your future career goals.

THRIVE WHERE YOU ARE

Leverage Opportunity Where You Are Now

CHAPTER *7*

HONOR YOUR STRENGTHS

I t's better to play to your strengths rather than try to fix your weaknesses. It's surprising how many continue to work against their own proverbial grain. You are not broken — you are extraordinary, just as you are, but you may be in a career that doesn't optimize your strengths.

Not everyone needs a complete overhaul to refresh and re-ignite their career engagement. Small hacks can help you re-discover what you love about your strengths and put them into practice so you can reinvigorate your work now.

Identify Your True Strengths

Are you in a job where you're regularly receiving feedback that doesn't validate you or your work? A job where you feel like you don't measure up? A job where you're being regularly questioned or cautioned about your performance or where you feel drained of energy all the time?

If you find yourself swimming upstream and dreading the workday, it's time to focus on what you can change. A great first step is identifying your strengths. When you know your strengths, you can focus on environments where you will thrive. The following steps can help you on the path to discovering your true strengths:

1. **Get feedback.** Ask those in your circle of trust for five things you do well. Of the answers you receive, think about the things you especially love — that energize you. Keep in mind that just because you do something well doesn't mean it's a true strength. It's the energy you feel for the endeavor that's key. You will compare the circle of trust feedback with your own reflections to identify what truly energizes you.

2. **Take a strengths assessment.** There are several instruments that can help you assess your strengths. My favorite is the CliftonStrengths Assessment, which you can do through a Gallup-Certified Strengths Coach, like me, or by going directly to the Gallup.com website. The assessment helps individuals and teams leverage their strengths to improve workplace engagement and well-being. When you are thriving in a role and playing to your strengths, your productivity and career satisfaction soar.

3. **Try a new approach.** Applying your newfound insights, look at your work life with fresh eyes. When you focus on your strengths, you tap into your innate talents (what you naturally do well), which leads to greater satisfaction in your career and life.

When you are in alignment with your strengths, you experience an expanding energy that excites you about your work. Rather than trying to swim upstream by attempting to fix your weaknesses and please others, focus on what really matters — finding happiness for yourself, which in turn helps those around you. Your work feels engaging and gratifying, and time tends to fly by. When you play to your strengths, you have a stronger sense of well-being, passion, and flow — often referred to as being "in the zone."

The Power of the Reframe

If you find yourself in a role where you are constantly being asked to improve or change, you owe it to yourself to consider whether this is the right place for you. It may be time to reframe your situation and find an opportunity that honors the strengths you are not using at present. You are not broken, after all — you are simply not in a role that showcases your natural talents.

Reframing allows you to invest your energy in a role where you can sharpen and polish your natural strengths rather than a role that focuses on competencies you don't have in abundance to begin with. The reframe helps you look on the bright side. It's focusing on the donut and not the hole; it's making the best of things and honoring the gifts and talents you possess.

In my TEDxWomen talk, I harkened back to the dark days when I was completely at loose ends after leaving my career as an opera singer. At the time, I knew I wanted to step away from the world of professional opera, but I had no idea how I would pursue a career in anything other than music. Gradually, by re-framing and looking at my career limbo through a new lens, I began to see the value in the skills I'd developed through my vocal training and performance experience. I began to see how those skills could be transferred into a new, non music-related profession. I started to focus on what I *had* rather than on what I'd lost. That vulnerability was my catalyst for change and empowered me on a new career path that I truly love.

Consider this Howard Thurman quote: "Don't ask yourself what the world needs. Ask yourself what makes you come alive and go do that because what the world needs is people who have come alive!"[4]

Autonomy, Mastery, and Purpose

Knowing your strengths is the first step. Knowing how your strengths impact and connect with the company mission is next and can enhance your feelings of connectedness and purpose at work. Whether you are a team member or a team leader, be sure to discuss how individuals and teams make an impact. Encourage colleagues to reflect upon and articulate their "Why?"

- Why do you work here?
- Why do you get out of bed each morning and come to work?

Having clarity about autonomy, mastery, and purpose feeds your engagement at work.

Autonomy – Have ownership of something you can take pride in and call your own accomplishment.

Mastery – Stretch and develop your skills with professional development or challenging new work to stimulate growth.

Purpose – Know how your work is part of the mission of the organization and gives you a sense of belonging.

Let the Love Back In

The global pandemic has been an awakening and focused a spotlight on career disengagement. Toxic work cultures, employee dissatisfaction, and few opportunities for advancement have resulted in a mass exit of people from their current jobs. Dubbed the Great Resignation, this movement highlights the importance of workplace culture and developing employees for future success.

I've been a longtime consumer of the research, thought leadership, and wisdom of Marcus Buckingham. He shows us how we can address these new challenges by rediscovering what we truly love in his book: *Love and Work: How to Find What You Love, Love What You Do, and Do It for the Rest of Your Life*.[5] Simply put, he advocates for people to spend most of each day at work using their greatest talents and engaging in their favorite tasks. By allowing people to do what they want and what they are good at, both the organization and the employees win.

Strengths are your inborn talents, which you can hone and polish to a level of self-mastery. Your strengths energize you and bring you satisfaction, and they can also help you find the right role or career that honors the best version of you.

Honoring your strengths will help you find joy and love in your work and your life. Living your strengths allows you to become the very best you.

As an executive coach, I hear from many clients who are unhappy either in their workplace or in their current roles. Because these are not honoring their strengths, they are on the brink of burnout or already fried.

Studies tell us that fewer than 16 percent of workers are fully engaged at work, and as Buckingham says, "The rest of us are just selling our time and our talent and getting compensated for our trouble."

It's time to focus on your strengths and make a change.

Intentionality

My client Jillian is an accomplished tax attorney and a partner in a large, distinguished law firm in Boston. By multiple measures, she is successful. She has cultivated an enviable book of business, earns a top salary with bonuses, and was promoted to partner with potential for continued growth in the firm. The problem is that Jillian doesn't love her work anymore. She is very good at tax law, but the work doesn't gratify her in the way that it did earlier in her career.

Imagine Jillian being sealed in her office for 12 hours a day, rarely interacting with people, and feeling chained to her desk, crunching tax code. She had lost her mojo and found no joy in her career — even though she was recognized for her work.

Just because you are good at something doesn't mean it energizes you. I encouraged Jillian to take the CliftonStrengths Assessment, and we discovered talents she was not optimizing. She spoke with the lead equity partners about taking on a more developmental role in the firm, setting strategy for long-term business development and lawyer retention. She pitched the idea of training the incoming newbie tax lawyers with a focus on the future of the organization and developing a talent succession plan.

The equity partners gave her a nine-month window to test-drive and prove this new role and quantify the return on their investment. She now interacts on a daily basis with other lawyers and stakeholders and has initiated a training and development program for the new tax lawyers to help them learn the ropes from a seasoned pro. She is thriving in the firm and loves flexing new intellectual muscles that she wasn't leveraging in her other role. Talent retention rates in the tax practice have grown by 26 percent, and Jillian is now taking her model to other practice groups in the firm. By her own admission, by bringing love back into her work, she's helping her law firm retain top talent, including her.

You can enjoy a successful career and live a rewarding life, but it takes intentionality to focus on doing what you do well and what energizes you.

PRO TIPS

- Get feedback, take an assessment, or experiment with something new to test-drive what energizes you and discover your true strengths.

- Consider the power of the reframe to look at new possibilities and reevaluate your career through a new lens.

- Reflect upon the power of autonomy, mastery, and purpose in your current or future career role and how it intersects with your WHY.

CHAPTER 8

ARE YOU A MULTIPLIER OR A DIMINISHER?

From the corporate arena to higher education to nonprofits, I have had many clients who struggled with bosses they felt were ineffective leaders. Were these leaders intelligent and talented people? Yes. Were they able to lead a team, motivate others, and empower professional development and success in their colleagues? In many cases, no.

While a small percentage of leaders are born, most are developed through formal and informal training programs. Many organizations and career sectors do not place enough emphasis on training impactful leaders, and this leads to discontent amongst the ranks and, ultimately, poor morale and low productivity. Some enlightened organizations invest in training and developing leaders, and I am a strong believer in the benefits of this transformational talent development.

To that end, I have long been a follower of Liz Wiseman, CEO of the Wiseman Group and bestselling author on leadership and talent development. In her book *Multipliers: How the Best Leaders Make Everyone Smarter*, Wiseman teaches valuable lessons for current and aspiring leaders interested in amplifying the capabilities of those with whom they work. [6]

The World Needs More Multipliers

So why do some leaders boost the mental IQ in a room, and others suck the mental life out of their employees? Wiseman categorizes leaders who generate these different outcomes as Multipliers and Diminishers.

During Wiseman's 17-plus years of leadership watching and developing talent at Oracle, she discovered that some leaders drain the intelligence and capabilities of the people around them. Their focus on their own intelligence and their narcissistic need to be the smartest person in the room had a diminishing effect on everyone around them. For them to look smart, other people had to look dumb or incompetent, and in turn, these Diminishers created a vacuum suck of all the creative energy in a room. Meeting times were doubled, and other people's ideas suffocated and died in their presence. From these so-called leaders, intelligence only flowed one way — from them to others.

The Multipliers, on the other hand, used their leadership intelligence in a much different way. They used their intelligence to amplify the capabilities of others on their team. People got smarter and better in their presence. Ideas flowed freely, and challenges were overcome. When these leaders walked into a room, the team's energy level went up, and difficult problems were solved because every team member had a say and was involved.

Empowering Others to Amplify Their Capabilities

Multipliers bring out the intelligence in others by building collective and viral genius in an organization. As noted in her book, Wiseman identifies five types of Multipliers:

1. The Talent Magnet: Attracts and optimizes talent
2. The Liberator: Requires people's best thinking
3. The Challenger: Extends challenges
4. The Debate Maker: Debates decisions
5. The Investor: Instills accountability

By extracting people's full capabilities, Multipliers challenge and encourage those around them and obtain great outcomes.

Diminishers, according to Wiseman, drain the intelligence, energy, and capability from the people around them. Growth suffers, team member retention drops, and innovation is squashed because the leader has to put their mark on everything.

Wiseman shares a success story about Bill Campbell, former CEO of Intuit, who fully admits that he is a recovered Diminisher. A courageous team member called him on his micromanaging, intelligence-draining leadership style and pleaded with him to give the team space to create ideas and solve problems. It was a hard lesson for Campbell to learn, but in the long run, it gave him the insight he needed to become a more effective leader.

He now subscribes to the philosophy of creating brilliance in others on his team by empowering them to succeed. This is a difficult lesson for many of today's unsuccessful leaders. Some don't have the professional development resources to learn to become Multipliers. Others don't have courageous team members who call them out on being ineffective leaders, so they continue to diminish, and dysfunctional teams plod along. If you work for a micromanager, I hope this inspires you to be proactive and introduce the concept of Multipliers and Diminishers in your workplace.

Are You an Accidental Diminisher?

Many leaders fall into what Wiseman calls the Accidental Diminisher group. These individuals are "... managers with the best of intentions, good people who think they are doing a good job leading. Accidental or not, the impact on their team is the same — Diminishers only get ½ of the true brainpower of their people."[7] These leaders unintentionally diminish the people they lead. Many are following popular management techniques but are still missing the mark.

Find Out if You're a Multiplier or a Diminisher

Wiseman created a free online quiz to help you find out how you might unintentionally diminish the people you lead. You can find it at TheWisemanGroup.com/Quiz.

The starting point for every leader should be self-awareness and a commitment to continuous self-actualization. This quiz will give you a safe space to discover if you are a Multiplier or a Diminisher and provide action steps to enhance your leadership so others can thrive working with you.

Work at becoming the leader who uses their intelligence to amplify the smarts and capabilities of the people around them. The world needs more Multipliers — especially when leaders are expected to do more with less.

PRO TIPS

- Reflect upon whether you are a Multiplier who uses your intelligence to amplify the capabilities of others on your team or a Diminisher who creates a vacuum suck of all the creative energy in a room by focusing on yourself.

- Focus on Wiseman's five disciplines of Multipliers:

  1. The Talent Magnet: Attracts and optimizes talent
  2. The Liberator: Requires people's best thinking
  3. The Challenger: Extends challenges
  4. The Debate Maker: Debates decisions
  5. The Investor: Instills accountability

CHAPTER 9

RECHARGE AND REIGNITE YOUR CAREER

The global economy is in a constant state of change. Mergers and acquisitions impact growth and can result in downsizing, which impacts hiring practices. People typically change careers by necessity or by choice. What's stopping you from changing now? Instead of waiting for the perfect time to take charge of your destiny or waiting for the perfect job to reignite your career and your life, choose to make a positive change now.

For many years, I held leadership roles in organizations that aligned with my values and advocated for missions I believed in. I worked with incredible colleagues and others who were in desperate need of leadership development. My coaching, speaking, and consulting practice was a side hustle that I "fit in," burning precious PTO days. While my private work truly energized me and filled my professional cup, I was tethered to my day job because of the usual gravity problems — steady income, healthcare, and retirement benefits. I dreamt of the day I would have the courage to take the leap and become a full-time entrepreneur, but my fears outweighed my courage.

What Are You Waiting For?

As the years went on, my private practice was calling to me, and the joy in that work outweighed the satisfaction I found working for a large company. I also knew that extricating myself from my current role would help me break my addictive work habits, which were being celebrated and encouraged. I was screaming inside and knew it was time to make a change.

I realized I was stuck in the debilitating mental loop of, "It will get better when..." and I was waiting for something that I might not even have been able to recognize. I spent more hours working than I spent living and enjoying my family, friends, and life. I was on the very same debilitating career treadmill that I had coached numerous clients to get off, and it was time to practice what I had been preaching.

After months of self-reflection, numerous pros and cons lists, and research into healthcare and retirement accounts, I decided to take the leap. After all, I was a seasoned career reinventor, having transitioned from the performing arts as an opera singer to the world of career and professional development. I was a leader who had scaled large ventures, led teams of people, and worked my way up to the rank of vice president. I was an executive coach; why was this so bloody hard for me?

I share my vulnerability with you because I know how hard it can be in the career world. I also know how hard it is to make a change that feels risky. As Brené Brown says, "Vulnerability is the birthplace of innovation, creativity and change."[8] It was only when I gave myself permission to be truly vulnerable that I gained the courage and bravery to take a step forward on an uncharted path that excited me greatly, even though it was terrifying.

It Starts with a Baby Step

Where you begin is up to you. Your next move might be a tweak, perhaps realigning into a role that showcases your strengths. Or, you may have a full-on reinvention that involves a career change or an entrepreneurial venture. Wherever you are, know that you can begin with small steps to get started on your journey. **The most important step is giving yourself permission to get started now and stop waiting for it to get better.**

Five Action Steps

As part of your professional refresh, there are five essential self-reflection action steps that will help you recharge and reignite your life and career. These steps will empower you with confidence and help you discover what you really want so you can gain momentum and work toward your goals.

1. **Consider What You Value** – Take time to get quiet with yourself and determine what you truly value. Values are the biggest predictor of career satisfaction. Rank the

things that are most important for you in a career, such as flexibility, security, autonomy, salary, work/life integration, etc. A values list can be endless, and only you can articulate what is important for your work environment. Keep in mind that values evolve and change over time, so what you want in a career now may be very different from the role you held five years ago or the one you'll have in five years.

2. **Rediscover Your Interests** – Knowing your interests can help you unlock possibilities when choosing a role or career. Interests are the biggest predictors in career selection since we gravitate toward what we like. Are you a hands-on doer, an investigative thinker, or someone who likes to create and invent? Perhaps you are interested in helping people or enjoy organizing data and information. Maybe you enjoy persuading and influencing others to achieve a goal. Reflect on your interests, and they may lead you to a new career or entrepreneurial opportunity.

3. **Embrace Your Personality** – Personality refers to your unique patterns of mental, emotional, physical, and behavioral characteristics. Your personality preferences play a big role in the types of work you may like or dislike. Consider the following questions:

   - Where do you draw your energy? Do you prefer to focus on the external world of people and actions, or are you energized by ideas and feelings of the inner world?
   - How do you perceive information? Do you focus on the realities of the present or the possibilities of the future?

- How do you make decisions? Are you guided by objective, analytical reasoning or subjective, personal values?
- What is your need for order in life? Do you prefer to be organized and planned or spontaneous and flexible?

Know thyself, and honor your inborn personality type to help find a career that matches your natural tendencies.

4. **Scrutinize Your Skill Set** – A skill is an ability, based on training or experience, to do something well. The goal is to discover what your skills are and market them with humble confidence to make you attractive to employers who value these skills in the workplace. Skills fall into three main categories:

    - **Transferable Skills** – These are taken from job to job and are important in many career sectors. Examples include communication (verbal and written), critical thinking, analytical, leadership, and teamwork.
    - **Specialized Knowledge** – These skills are relevant to a particular job or career field. Examples include operating laboratory equipment, computer coding, and foreign language abilities.
    - **Adaptive Skills** – These skills encompass the personal competencies you bring to the professional environment and are often the most sought after by employers. Examples include emotional intelligence, motivation, initiative, integrity, flexibility, and resilience.

5. **Develop Your Brand** – You must showcase your strengths and define your superpowers. Market your unique combination of interests and talents, and develop your story about

why you are a valuable commodity. If you need a jump start, query people in your circle of trust and ask them what makes you special. Ultimately, you are in control of your personal brand, but gathering input from others can be a great point of departure.

Take the time to get quiet with yourself and discover what you value, what interests you, how your personality plays a role in your career, and inventory your skills. You can't plan your career road map until you know where you want to go, and it begins with self-reflection.

Whether you are looking to reinvent yourself in the same industry, transition to a new career, or develop your own business, this is your opportunity to clean the slate and design a new professional persona that plays to your strengths and feeds your soul so you can take control of your career and your life.

Onward to new beginnings because life will pass you by if you wait for things to get better.

PRO TIPS

- Get vulnerable and dig deep to reflect on your happiness and satisfaction in your life and career.

- Consider what you value – Take the time to get quiet with yourself and determine what matters.

- Rediscover your interests – Knowing your interests can help you unlock possibilities when considering a change.

- Embrace your personality – Identifying your unique patterns of mental, emotional, physical, and behavioral characteristics helps focus your efforts.

- Scrutinize your skill set – Define your abilities, based on training or experience, to do something well.

- Identify your superpowers – Identify your unique combination of interests and talents and develop your story about why you are a valuable commodity.

CHAPTER 10

EXECUTIVE PRESENCE AND AWARENESS

Executive presence used to hark back to images of senior corporate employees in expensive business suits who exerted influence in lavish offices and boardrooms. Nowadays, savvy organizations have a much broader understanding of executive presence. They've destigmatized remote work, the dress code has skewed casual, and the hybrid workplace is becoming the new expectation for much of the global workforce.

With a multigenerational workforce navigating the world of work together, executive presence remains important, but the rules of engagement have changed for the better. It's now less about the business suit and more about engaging with others in a way that gives them confidence in your leadership abilities. Navigating these new terms will set you up for success.

The New Executive Presence

Even seasoned leaders can benefit from freshening up their executive presence and should never take how others perceive them for granted.

Executive presence is your ability to inspire confidence in others. From your subordinates and peers to the top of the food chain, your ability to believe in yourself and enthuse others will distinguish you. If advancement and growth are part of your career plan, executive presence will help you become recognized for your accomplishments and showcase your added value in a palatable way.

Dress Code

Dressing for success will always resonate in the world of work, even if your organizational culture is casual. I have executive clients in the tech world who say that dressing up means wearing socks. I'm not suggesting you need to wear a suit to be seen and heard but evaluate the impression you want to make and dress accordingly, honoring the culture where you work.

In our Zoom-meeting-dominated world, proper lighting, a pleasing background, and appropriate clothing impact how you are perceived. When you have in-person meetings, be mindful of your head-to-toe attire and personal grooming. Casual Friday has taken on a new meaning, and while work-from-home comfort is a perk for many, being too casual can send a message you may not want associated with your personal brand.

Practice Your Body Language

I'm fascinated by nonverbal signals communicated through body language. Be aware of how you make eye contact (even on Zoom) and check your posture. Good posture exudes confidence, and eye contact signals active listening. Facial expressions convey emotion and can be easily misinterpreted, so ask a trusted friend or colleague to give you candid feedback.

"Resting Bitch Face" (RBF) now has a Wikipedia page and is defined as a facial expression that "unintentionally appears as if a person is angry, annoyed, irritated, or contemptuous, particularly when the individual is relaxed, resting, or not expressing any emotion." [9] While this may seem benign and humorous, our facial expressions have psychological implications regarding bias, stereotypes, judgment, and decision-making. Do an RBF check and be aware of how others perceive your facial expression!

Check Your Emotional Baggage

Leaders with heightened executive presence tap their emotional intelligence and steer away from the drama that occurs in every work setting. Avoid the gossip and the grapevine, and honor your colleagues with empathy, knowing that everyone has bad days when the challenges of life impact our work.

Practice staying calm and maintain levelheaded leadership, especially when emotions are running high and those around you lose their composure. Your ability to navigate your stress by sticking with the facts and listening to both sides of every story will empower you to lead with a trusted and respected executive voice.

Cultivate Your Leadership Voice

It's not what you say but how you convey your message that ensures it lands for each audience. Context is essential. It's important to know your audience and customize each message to be relevant, compelling, and sticky enough to be memorable.

Take time to reach out to at least one person each week outside of your immediate team or functional area. Try to learn how they fit into the business and organization. Learn about their goals and challenges and ways you might support them as a strategic partner.

Leaders with executive presence think strategically about how to solve problems, lead with solutions, and inspire a vision to bring others into the fold. Executive presence reflects your behavior, not just your wardrobe.

Brand Audit

Before you develop or refresh your executive presence, you must gain clarity about how you are perceived by others in your workplace and beyond. I recommend a personal brand audit where you ask a handful of people in your circle of trust to share honest feedback about how you are seen, heard, and perceived in the workplace.

I start my brand audit participants with the question, "What do others say about me when I am not in the room?

This can help you create a new narrative, if needed, or double down on what you are doing well to keep your executive presence strong. Only ask those who are prepared and willing to give you developmental feedback that addresses your blind spots. A professional coach can help you navigate this journey if you need an objective point of view. A recorded Zoom meeting can also be a great way to observe yourself in action.

Find a Role Model

Be observant of other leaders in your realm who you admire. What is it about the way they speak, comport themselves, or lead that you find compelling? Identify these traits and characteristics and make them your own. Perhaps you are modeling the way for someone else who admires your executive presence.

Confidence Comes in Many Forms

There is an American cultural bias that favors extraverts, especially those who are dynamic and charismatic. If this is part of your authentic persona, celebrate it but be cognizant not to overwhelm and be diligent about honing your active listening skills.

There are many introverted leaders with exceptional executive presence. Being an internal processor is a trait to be commended, but it's often misunderstood. I encourage incredible introverts to be seen and heard in ways that honor their style and help others know they are 100 percent in the conversation, even if they are not the first to respond or the loudest voice in the room.

True confidence comes with humility and vulnerability. The best executive presence comes from a place of authenticity, so you can be comfortable in your own skin and leverage your individual strengths.

Find your own signature style and celebrate it as the core of your executive presence. Honor what sets you apart and how you want others to perceive you. Executive presence gives you clout and credibility in the world of work and can be a distinguishing factor in your upward mobility.

PRO TIPS

- Hone your emotional intelligence to showcase your leadership persona and how you treat others.

- Conduct a brand audit to learn how others perceive you and adjust accordingly if your persona is misunderstood.

- Find a role model you admire to emulate in behavior and communication and develop your style with these traits in mind.

- Cultivate your leadership voice to showcase your influence, honoring your introversion or extraversion personality type.

- Virtual executive presence includes good lighting, eye contact, and the appropriate background that does not pull focus.

CHAPTER **11**

CONSIDER WHAT TO KEEP & STOP

As an executive coach, I work with many individuals who are stalled or stuck in a stagnant routine of life and career that zaps their energy and enthusiasm.

I have an exercise called **Keep & Stop** that can transform your world by helping you clarify and define what's important to you on a personal and/or professional level. The **Keep & Stop** reflection will help you unpack what's working, what's not working, and what you need to make your life better.

Less Is More

Think of the Keep & Stop as a reset. You're taking time to reflect on what works, what's zapping your energy or not working, and where you want to go. I interviewed author Leidy Klotz on my

Your Working Life podcast, and he takes an innovative approach to improving lives with a less-is-more paradigm shift. [10] This concept is useful to consider before sitting down and doing the reflection. Klotz notes:

> We pile on "to-dos" but don't consider "stop-doings." We create incentives for good behavior but don't get rid of obstacles to it. We collect new-and-improved ideas but don't prune the outdated ones. Every day, across challenges big and small, we neglect a basic way to make things better: we don't subtract.

Leidy Klotz's pioneering research shows that our minds tend to add before taking away. Even when we make a conscious effort to streamline, it's harder to subtract things because an array of biological, cultural, and economic forces push us toward more. But we have a choice — our blind spot need not go on taking a toll on our cities, institutions, or minds. By diagnosing our neglect of subtraction, we can treat it.

We need to foster a less-is-more paradigm shift that exemplifies how removing something can lead to better outcomes. We rarely give ourselves permission to remove things from our lives or careers but doing so can make things better. When we overlook subtraction, we tend toward overwhelm, overwork, and being overextended.

Keep & Stop Reflection

With a less-is-more mindset, it's time to carve out some reflection time and consider the **Keep & Stop** exercise. I suggest you discuss your findings with a trusted friend, mentor, or coach who can help you activate your plan and provide support and accountability.

Find a notebook and pen, head to a quiet place, and let's get started.

1. **Keep**. Identify the things that strengthen your career and/or personal life. These are things you want to continue to do. This is positive pattern recognition. What are you doing that is having a powerful impact on your life and career? **Spend some time journaling your *Keep* intentions.**

2. **Stop**. Successful leaders are effective and quick when it comes to recognizing negative patterns. Ask yourself if there are any thorns in your side — any frustrations you keep having to deal with? Any counterproductive measures you could eliminate or change? What has a negative impact on your career or personal life? **Journal your *Stop* intentions.**

Getting Unstuck

Change in life is constant and comes by choice or necessity. While you always have the power to design a new path on your personal journey or create a life and career that brings you meaning and fulfillment, it can be easy to get stuck. I've worked with many clients who want a change, but it seems overwhelming. Oftentimes, they don't know where to begin, so I get them started by having them work through the following questions:

1. Am I being my authentic self in my career and personal life? If not, what is holding me back?
2. What would I do less of if I had the option?
3. What would I do if I were not afraid? What do I need to do to make this a reality?

Designing your future is not a linear process or one-solution endeavor, and you need not do it alone. Ask for help and provide help in return. There is no shame in asking others for help, especially when it's to create a future that better aligns with your values, interests, and strengths. Having the courage to reach out to those you trust and ask them to support you on the journey may reveal that others are also on a quest to design a new future. Having a support system is empowering.

Start with trusted colleagues or mentors who have seen your work in action. Ask them to share what they see as your strengths and potential. Consider working with a career or executive coach to help you gain better self-awareness and create an action plan for your goals and aspirations. Tapping the insights of others can help you work around your blind spots and consider things you may have never thought possible.

Input from others will help you gain clarity and focus. But remember to honor what you want and have the courage to define success on your own terms. Don't put limits on your design plans and give yourself permission to test-drive multiple new options. Most success happens after a myriad of trials and errors and failing forward. Think like an entrepreneur and learn the art of recovery and resilience.

Don't let the inertia of life carry you into the future. Regain your control and design the future you can enjoy — and consider what you can subtract.

PRO TIPS

- The less-is-more paradigm shift exemplifies how removing something can lead to better design.

- **Keep** – Identify and continue to do the things that strengthen your career and/or personal life.

- **Stop** – Identify and eliminate or change counter-productive actions.

- Don't let the inertia of life carry you into the future.

- Regain control and design the future you can enjoy — and consider what you can subtract.

CHALLENGES THAT SUCK

Let's Get Real; Shit Happens

CHAPTER 12

APPROACH CONFLICT WITH A COACHING MINDSET

Navigating the good, the bad, and the ugly of workplace relationships can be exhausting. This section digs deep into what's really happening at work that nobody wants to talk about — but should! Clear away the dysfunction for solutions you can work with.

Most of us have experienced an uncomfortable situation with a colleague at work that resulted in conflict, heightened emotions, or ideological differences. While some conflict-averse individuals use avoidance to sweep problems under the rug, that technique doesn't solve the issue and often results in festering thoughts and rumination that is emotionally debilitating.

While addressing conflict may seem daunting, approaching the dysfunction with a coaching mindset will help you create a healthier work environment that supports open communication, psychological safety, and cognitive diversity. We don't always have to agree with each other, but we can model professional behavior by treating people with dignity and respect.

Assume Positive Intent

Disappointment, mistakes, and failures happen on every team, and the knee-jerk reaction is often to blame or shame. We often judge the mistakes of another more harshly than our own, but this behavior can be changed. To assume positive intent, we can begin by giving people the benefit of the doubt and believing they had good intentions. Identify the situational facts and get the details of the bigger picture before jumping to conclusions.

Leading with curiosity about intention is a healthier way to communicate and changes the confrontational approach to a listening and learning opportunity. This diffuses emotions on both sides and works toward establishing or deepening trust.

Check Your Emotions at the Gate

You can't logic your way through emotions, but you can recognize your emotional triggers and better understand how to manage your professional communication and composure, so your message honors the content you wish to share and not the rollercoaster feelings you may be experiencing.

Difficult conversations are tough, so process the emotions in a space that honors your psychological safety. If you communicate with heightened emotions, it changes how people remember what you say.

Clear Is Kind

The goal of addressing conflict is to honor the input of both parties and work toward a resolution. You must clarify your own interests and that of the other person.

Brené Brown comes to mind with her "Clear is Kind. Unclear is Unkind." philosophy from her book, *Dare to Lead*.[11] Some leaders avoid tough conversations, including giving honest, productive feedback. Brown's research found that the cultural norm of being "nice and polite" led to a lack of clarity and shared purpose that resulted in unresolved conflicts, diminished trust and engagement, increased problematic behavior, and decreased performance.

Brown further clarifies kind and unkind behavior in the following passage:

> Feeding people half-truths or bullshit to make them feel better (which is almost always about making ourselves feel more comfortable) is unkind. Not getting clear with a colleague about your expectations because it feels too hard yet holding them accountable or blaming them for not delivering is unkind.

Recognizing that real conversations can be tough, Brown offers the Rumble technique to get the dialogue started.

Let's Rumble

At the heart of every conflict are misalignment and a lack of clarity. If we open our hearts and our minds to have courageous conversations and lead with the vulnerability of "I'm wrestling with this ..." it breaks down the barrier of them versus us and puts both parties on the same page.

Brown calls these types of conversations a Rumble and defines them as follows:

> A Rumble is a discussion, conversation, or meeting defined by a commitment to lean into vulnerability, to stay curious and generous, to stick with the messy middle of problem identification and solving, to take a break and circle back when necessary, to be fearless in owning our parts, and, as psychologist Harriet Lerner teaches, to listen with the same passion with which we want to be heard.

Some helpful Rumble conversation starters include:

- I'm curious about
- Tell me more
- That's not my experience
- I'm wondering
- Help me understand
- Walk me through this
- What's your passion around this?
- Tell me why this doesn't fit/work for you

Listen More, Talk Less

No matter how thin the pancake is, there are always two sides. While we know there are two sides to every story, it's easy to jump into blaming and shaming. Active listening is essential here and allows for an open mind until all the information is on the table to consider.

Approach the conversation with curiosity and lead with cues like "Tell me more..." or "Did I understand you correctly?" and restate what you heard. It's not unusual to have conflict scenarios involving more than a single person, so let everyone participate and have their say.

Accountability is important and owning your part in the conflict creates a culture that makes it safe to fail forward. Have the humility to own your mistakes and approach what's next with a growth mindset, no matter what side of the conflict you are on. Each party has an opportunity to grow and learn from the conflict.

Clarify Next Steps

Identifying a common goal or resolution is the most desirable outcome for resolving a conflict. You must first identify the root cause or issue that led to the problem. And ideally, both sides will come together to discover how to work toward a common goal or resolution to their original issue.

Solution generation is the best part of conflict resolution because both parties come together to generate ideas or compromises that are agreed upon. The goal is to find common ground or an idea that is acceptable to both parties. Compromise and negotiation are opportunities to practice the art of the possible with a fresh start and a commitment by both parties to keeping the lines of communication open.

Great leaders know how to listen with curiosity, assume positive intent, and bring a healthy Rumble to work through conflict. These skills can be honed and take a commitment to continuous growth and development.

PRO TIPS

- Assume positive intent when disappointment, mistakes, and failures happen.

- Difficult conversations are uncomfortable, so process emotions in a safe space that honors your psychological safety.

- Honor Brené Brown's "Clear is Kind. Unclear is Unkind." philosophy.

- Learn to Rumble and lean into vulnerability; stay curious and generous and stick with the messy middle of a problem.

- Listen more, talk less.

- Clarify the next steps.

CHAPTER 13

BRAVE, NOT PERFECT

With social media permeating our daily lives, things can seem pretty freakin' perfect out there. In this Instagram world, where photos are filtered and flawless and family and friends seem to be having the times of their lives, it's easier than ever to fall into the "perfect" trap.

Striving for perfection is different than striving for a goal. Perfection, by definition, is something that is "free from fault and defect."[12] That's impossible. We're all perfectly imperfect and trying to attain perfection naturally leaves many of us feeling stuck and unable to move forward.

I've seen many of my executive coaching clients struggle with the notion of perfection. Working together, I've helped them let go of perfect and develop new ways to attain growth and success.

Bravery Deficit

In her book, *Brave, Not Perfect,* Reshma Saujani, founder and CEO of Girls Who Code, says women are far more affected by the perfection affliction than men. She contends that this drive to do things right or not at all can be a huge barrier to success.[13]

In her TED Talk on which her book is based, Saujani says this conditioning starts young. She makes the case that, early on, girls are taught to smile pretty, be nice, get all As, and generally play it safe in life — which causes them to hold back if they don't feel they can perform perfectly. She points out that boys, on the other hand, are conditioned and encouraged to play rough and tough, swing high, and generally dive headfirst into life — making them more comfortable with failure and risk-taking.

"We're raising our girls to be perfect and our boys to be brave," Saujani laments in her TED Talk. "Some people worry about our federal deficit, but I worry about our bravery deficit. We're losing out because we're not raising our girls to be brave." [14] Saujani contends that this bravery deficit is why women have historically been so underrepresented in STEM, C-suites, boardrooms, and Congress.

I've certainly seen this bravery deficit play out in my executive coaching practice — from the types of jobs my clients will consider to the degree to which they feel they'll be successful in a particular job to the interview process itself. When clients start to fall into this paralyzing perfection trap, I work with them to move forward — even though the steps may feel messy, imperfect, and a bit risky.

"The socialization of perfection has caused us to take less risks in our careers," Saujani explains, "... it means our economy is being left behind on all the innovation and problems women would solve if they were socialized to be brave."

Here are some of my favorite myth-busting reminders that perfection is overrated (adapted from *Brave, Not Perfect*). I encourage you to stick these on your fridge or vision board and read them often:

1. **Failure is allowed.**
2. **Perfect does not equal happy.**
3. **Things won't fall apart if I'm not perfect.**
4. **Perfection does not equal excellence.**
5. **I can make mistakes and still be successful.**

Facing Your Fears

By facing our fears, allowing imperfection, finding courage, and taking risks, we open ourselves up to new growth and success that wouldn't otherwise have been possible. I encourage you to let go of perfect and find the courage to go for what you really want in life. Here are some ways to get started.

Look for Your Ledge – Chances are there's at least one challenge, one change, one dream quietly calling out to you that you're afraid to step up to. It's a scary thing — the thing that, if you could do it, would make a major change in your life. Figure out what your scary thing is and move toward it.

Get Caught Trying – The best way to become fearless is to walk into the fire of fear and get used to challenging yourself as often as possible. Take risks. As the saying goes, better to have tried and failed than not to have tried at all.

Get Comfortable with Failure and Rejection – In the startup innovation world, there's a well-known saying: Fail forward — fast and often. Entrepreneurs seek out rejection to learn and improve their products or service in a speedy and efficient manner. In Silicon Valley, no one takes you seriously until you have multiple failure and recovery stories to tell. Learning that failure is feedback can help you adjust course and develop perseverance — an important attribute when moving forward with bravery.

All of these challenges encourage you to let go of the debilitating mindset, "I'll be ready when ..." and focus on what you can do now. They give you a chance to focus on working toward your personal best and getting comfortable with being a lifelong work in progress. Striving for perfection or waiting for absolute readiness is a waste of precious energy, and who has time for that?

Prototype, Test, Repeat

Getting stuck often equals being fearful about the unknowns on the other side of an equation. To help my executive coaching clients try new things and potentially figure out what's on the other side of a decision, I rely on a methodology called design thinking — a creative, iterative approach to problem-solving that helps people make well-informed decisions.

Design thinking is human-centered and gives people an opportunity to try new things, test their ideas, and get feedback. I can personally vouch for this technique since I used design thinking to help me take the entrepreneurial leap to running my consulting business.

The design thinking process involves the following steps:

1. **Ideation** – Brainstorm questions and multiple creative ideas for what you want to do.
2. **Prototyping** – Create a potential solution and prepare a representation of one or more of the ideas to show others. Think of it as a rough draft.
3. **Feedback** – Share the prototype with your professional circle of trust and ask for feedback. What worked? What didn't?
4. **Repeat** – Repeat this process with as many new concepts as you are considering. You'll gain valuable insights by crowdsourcing feedback.

The process is, by nature, forward-moving and gives you opportunities to turn ideas into prototypes and, eventually, reality.

Good Enough to Go

At some point, you have to decide that a project is "good enough to go." Seasoned designers relish this phrase because they know that, in most cases, you can basically continue to refine and tweak a concept, product, or idea forever. Think of the Apple iPhone and its many iterations. I am confident there will be more to come. Rarely is something absolutely done.

The ideation and prototyping phases of the design thinking process tap into the "good enough to go" energy by not requiring anything to be 100 percent refined or polished. Ideation gives you permission to come up with multiple creative solutions to prototype and eventually test. At this point, Big Hairy Audacious Goals (BHAG) are encouraged! More on these later.

When I took the leap from working for an organization to running my own consulting practice, I put "good enough to go" to the test. I surrendered to the reality that I'd never be 100 percent ready for anything, and I was willing to learn as I went and continuously improve with a growth mindset. If I had waited for what I thought "ready" looked like, I would still be suffering the workaholic lifestyle I enabled. Taking the risk and moving forward was the best investment in myself and my business.

Keep It Simple

People often get stuck in the perfection trap. They get overwhelmed and just shut down. Instead, release the idea of perfect and embrace the imperfections that make life interesting.

Leverage imperfection, take more risks, and work to build your courage, so you can build a better world for yourself. Here's to moving forward with bravery rather than perfectionism into a courageous new world!

PRO TIPS

- Ask yourself, "What would I do to make my life better if I were not afraid?" Move toward that answer.

- The best way to become fearless is to walk into the fire of fear and get used to challenging yourself as often as possible. Take risks.

- Fail forward — fast and often. Understand that failure is just feedback that can help you adjust course and develop perseverance.

- By facing fears, allowing imperfection, finding courage, and taking risks, you open yourself up to new growth and success that wouldn't otherwise have been possible.

CHAPTER **14**

THE "NO JERKS" POLICY

I have worked with countless employers seeking best-fit candidates to fill critical leadership roles in their organizations. In all industries, recruiters and hiring managers agree that after the basic criteria of skills and competencies are met, candidates are accepted or eliminated based on how well they fit into the culture of an organization. Savvy workplaces consider potential just as much as the skill set of a candidate, but nobody wants to hire a jerk, even if they are brilliant.

Working with people on internal teams and dealing with external stakeholders requires self-actualization and a keen awareness of how you fit into the dynamics of an organization. One bad apple can disrupt a work environment and wreak havoc on communication, trust, and collegial relationships — not to mention productivity. Protecting your team with a "No Jerks" hiring policy is smart and goes a long way to cultivating and preserving a harmonious and high-functioning workplace.

What qualities define a good colleague? Whether you are the candidate or the hiring manager, consider these attributes that distinguish a sought-after career mensch.

Communication 101

Organizations are like families when you consider how much time you spend together at work. A roller coaster of emotions occurs when any group of humans interacts to tackle challenges and create solutions. Effective communication is essential in order to keep the work-family as functional as possible.

- **Active listening** is a way to validate your colleagues and honor their thoughts and ideas with your full attention. Listen with your body language and your ears.

- **Recognizing colleagues** for a job well done can create and sustain a culture of advocacy. Be specific when sharing kudos since the ubiquitous "good job" doesn't resonate like specific feedback that highlights exactly how the individual earned your praise.

- **Less can be more when speaking.** Consider the value you bring to the table when speaking and focus on what's most important to the conversation. Succinct, clear, and germane communication is always well received.

- **Levity in the workplace** can ease tensions and build rapport but keep it clean and appropriate for your audience. A sense of humor can also foster a fun and positive workplace where people enjoy each other and the tasks at hand.

Agree to Disagree

High-functioning teams are made up of professionals with diverse ideas, different work styles, and varied personalities. Cast your team with people NOT like you and know that it's okay to disagree. Diverse perspectives make for engaging conversations that can lead to progressive change and innovation. Strong teams must learn how to communicate during times of both solidarity and disagreement. The art of compromise and negotiation always achieves the best result.

Additionally, having the humility to admit when you are wrong or have made a mistake goes a long way toward creating a sense of trust and accountability in a team.

Have the Backs of Your Colleagues

Building trust in the workplace is often the most difficult thing to achieve. Start with transparency and being true to your word. Do what you say you will do and be accountable for your actions. The most revered leaders have the backs of their colleagues and exhibit loyalty to the team, both in-house and with external constituents.

Be willing to step in to help others in need. Behave like a leader even if your job description does not reflect this status. Good colleagues help each other. Lending a hand to someone in need will create a culture that encourages others to help you when you need it most.

Let It Go

Stress is inevitable in the workplace, and how you behave under stress is something you should be aware of. I often ask candidates in an interview, "How does your behavior at work change when you are under stress?" Stress happens, and each person handles it differently. Approach stress with a beginner's mindset, and let it go like children do after a playground kerfuffle, so emotions don't fester and linger.

Be an Ambassador for Your Company

Whether you are at work or enjoying time away, you are always a representative of your organization. Consider how you are seen and heard beyond the walls of your organization, and always take the high road and speak professionally about your colleagues and clients. Even if you leave a company because of the boss from hell — speak respectfully about this person when asked in the new job interview. Dissing your old boss is never appropriate.

How Can I Help You?

Smart professionals ask for help. You should not avoid asking for something when you need it or refuse help when it's offered. This is especially true for new professionals and emerging leaders. Asking for help or clarification is not a weakness but a sign of self-confidence and humility.

The best leaders also regularly make themselves available to others. Be aware of how you can help colleagues and consider carving out 30 minutes each day to assist someone else in your workplace. This generous offer to help another will distinguish you as a leader and a generous professional.

Eccentric but Civil

There are some eccentric professionals out there whose behavior is not the norm, yet they are high functioning in a work environment. Bring on the quirky, eccentric, and odd — I celebrate different personas in the workplace if each person honors the common denominator of treating colleagues with dignity and respect. Lack of civility in the workplace is a deal breaker. The talent pool is deep with competitive candidates, and everyone is replaceable. Earning a job opportunity is a privilege, and unless you are a solo entrepreneur working in a vacuum, the "No Jerk" policy applies to everyone.

Jerk Rehabilitation

For those currently working with jerks, rest assured that some are salvageable. An executive coach can solicit stakeholder-centered feedback to illustrate how said jerk is perceived in the workplace. They can then enlighten them about their destructive behaviors and create an action plan to hone emotional intelligence.

While you can't put new ideas into an old mindset or achieve new results with old behaviors, a willing participant can adjust if they are inclined to grow.

PRO TIPS

- When hiring, consider potential as well as skill and establish a "No Jerks" policy to set expectations to treat all with dignity and respect.

- Hone your active listening skills, recognize the great work of others, and have the backs of your colleagues.

- Acknowledge that some people are eccentric and quirky and celebrate their individuality, but lack of civility should be a dealbreaker when hiring.

- Consider how you are seen and heard beyond the walls of your organization as a company ambassador.

CHAPTER **15**

THERE IS NO MIND READING AT WORK

Since many important career decisions are made when you are not in the room — like a new role, a promotion, or a plum assignment — it's essential to be seen and heard and to assert your intentions with clarity. Don't jeopardize your career future by assuming your boss understands your professional goals. Discover how to leverage your influence and leave mind reading to the psychics.

Gone are the days when working hard was enough to earn recognition or a promotion. To get ahead now, you need to take control of your career trajectory and design your own unique path. When mapping out your career future, be sure to tap into the wisdom of those who can help you to achieve those goals. Keeping your professional ambitions a well-kept secret will not move you forward. In this chapter, I'll cover some techniques I use with my executive coaching clients to prepare and position them for success.

Your Boss Is Not Your Career Coach

Many professionals naively believe their boss is committed to helping them advance. While this may happen with some extraordinary leaders, most bosses are focused on their own career future and are so busy doing their job that they may not recognize your achievements and value-add to the company. Sadly, it's often the problematic employees who get more attention than top performers.

Instead of faulting your boss for not being a mind reader, be clear and intentional. Share your aspirations, especially if you seek advancement or a change within the organization. Frequent and brief check-ins could change the relationship and help your boss become your advocate.

Consider working with an executive coach to create an action plan you can present to your boss. Clear goals and measurable outcomes will make it easier for your boss to champion you.

Manage Up

Managing up is the best way to let your boss know how your contributions are positively impacting the company. Don't wait for the annual performance review. Instead, reach out regularly via a brief email to communicate what you have accomplished as well as a few stretch goals. Be clear that no response is required, so this does not add to your boss's workload. You're demonstrating your accomplishments and making your achievements known. It's rare that great work is celebrated.

Develop Your Purple Cow

Global branding guru Seth Godin talks about the necessity of being remarkable. He argues that the only way to cut through the clutter of a crowded market is to innovate something new, unique, and remarkable, like a purple cow, which is Godin's signature image.

Marketing is not just for products or companies. Individuals need to consider how they are seen and heard in the career space and control the message they are sending out into the world. What makes you stand out in a crowd of competent professionals? Knowing your superpowers and showcasing them in the career world will make you indispensable and highly recruitable.

You have much more control of your life and career if you take ownership of the design process and broadcast your message.

What Is Being Said When You Are Not in the Room?

Most important decisions that happen in your career occur when you are not in the room. From the hiring decision to the bonus or salary increase, the powers that be discuss these matters without you in the room to self-advocate.

It's imperative that you recognize this and actively manage up your value to your immediate boss as well as other influencers and stakeholders in your organization who have the power to make career-altering decisions. Earn the trust and respect of ambassadors and sponsors who can promote your value and significance in the workplace to ensure that the decision-makers know why you are indispensable.

Leverage Your Influence

Just being squeaky isn't enough. The *way* you communicate your value-add message determines how you are perceived as a professional with influence.

- **Be seen and heard.** Go beyond your department, and share your subject matter expertise and professional superpowers where they can be leveraged.

- **Impact change.** Change is constant in every industry, so be seen as a change agent for good and embrace change with positivity and an open mind.

- **Provide solutions.** Bring suggestions, answers, and exploratory options to the table when complicated scenarios arise. There is no room for complaining when leveraging your influence.

Take a Seat at the Table

It takes courage and conviction to be seen and heard in your workplace. Communicate in creative ways, so your ideas are known beyond your individual rung on the company ladder.

Celebrate the diversity of thought and increase your visibility by having a voice in ways that distinguish you. If you are a remote worker, your digital presence is very important, so don't let out-of-sight be out-of-mind. Go the extra mile to impact positive change.

Own Your Power

Power is not given; it's taken. Too many people relinquish their power and let others make the most impactful career decisions about their future. Don't assume you know what someone else is thinking. No one is a mind reader. You need to keep your power by advocating for yourself. To this end, practice the following:

1. **Listen Up** – Walk in another's shoes and be sensitive to their unique perspective.

2. **Show Up** – Be present and engaged.

3. **Speak Up** – Have a point of view and be willing to entertain diversity of thought to discover new solutions.

4. **Brave Up** – Advocate for yourself and others and create a culture of trust.

Write Your Dream Job Description

My client Madison was stuck in a rut in her executive director role and aspired to advance to a vice president position in her organization. She was a classic high achiever, and because she didn't cause any trouble, her boss left her alone and sparingly praised her for a job well done. Madison knew her potential was barely being tapped, so I encouraged her to write a future job description to showcase what she wanted to do and to be clear about the expertise and potential she brought to the firm. She knew there were pain points at the firm that were not being addressed, and she was eager to and capable of tackling them.

Over several months, Madison did research with other senior leaders in the firm to make herself more visible and showcase what she did well to create a positive buzz beyond her current team. She learned about firmwide challenges, then created a proposal with her new job description and pitched it to her boss for consideration.

Her boss was surprised and reached out to the other leaders Madison had approached and heard the praise and appreciation about this ambitious, forward-thinking leader whom they had recently come to know. Her boss admitted that he had no idea Madison felt underutilized and was ready to take on a more complex role. It took several months, but in the new fiscal year, Madison's role was approved. She is thriving as a vice president in a company she really enjoys because she was proactive and made it clear to decision-makers that she was an asset to the firm by solving business pain points and providing valuable solutions. Retaining and promoting Madison was a win-win for her and the firm.

Design Your Career Destiny

To be in control of your career destiny, you must be proactive. Revisit your goals and adjust them as your life and career change. Ask for what you need from others and earn the support of sponsors who can champion your great work.

Setting yourself up to be successful requires you to be gritty, tenacious, and clear about what you want and to know what you do extraordinarily well. Don't fall prey to the myth that others know what you want in your career. Write down your intentions, share them with others, and coach those around you to do the same.

PRO TIPS

- Manage up your value-add to your boss and other influencers who have the power to make career-altering decisions.

- Know your superpowers and showcase them to make yourself indispensable and highly recruitable.

- Own your power: Listen Up, Show Up, Speak Up, and Brave Up, so others know your value.

- Don't fall prey to the mind-reading trap. Set yourself up to be successful by being clear about what you want with the leadership level above you.

- Take control of your career destiny by being proactive.

CHAPTER 16

GET REAL
WITH FEEDBACK

I work with leaders in all industries who struggle with giving developmental feedback and sharing recognition to celebrate the work of their direct reports. Feedback is almost always a one-way street with a top-down delivery system. It's time to democratize giving and receiving feedback. It's a skill everyone can develop and will result in better engagement, growth, and development for all.

Radical Candor

Kim Scott details how to give effective feedback in her book *Radical Candor: How to Be a Kick-Ass Boss Without Losing Your Humanity.* She advises that the more straightforward and honest those conversations can be, the better — not only during the review process but as a matter of course throughout the year.[15]

Scott drives home the case for straightforward honesty, explaining that while the truth can sometimes hurt, holding back the truth in a work situation is, in the long run, doing a disservice to your employees.

Scott's radical candor epiphany came during her tenure at Google when, after knocking a presentation to CEO Eric Schmidt out of the park, Scott's boss at the time, Sheryl Sandberg, asked her to meet.

Scott assumed Sandberg would be singing her praises (after all, her sales were beyond impressive); however, Sandberg pulled Scott aside for another reason. After some complimentary words, Sandberg let Scott know she'd been consistently interjecting "ums" throughout her presentation and went so far as to offer her a speech coach to help.

Scott was completely flummoxed by this. She'd given hundreds of presentations over the course of her career, and nobody had ever mentioned the "ums." When Scott brushed the observation off as just an inconsequential verbal tic, Sandberg realized she needed to be far more direct, "When you say 'um' every third word, it makes you sound stupid and insecure." This brought Scott to a full stop.

Sandberg now had Scott's full attention, and she went on to get the coaching that helped her eliminate "ums" from her presentations. While it pulled her up short at the time, Scott appreciated the fact that Sandberg got real with her — helping her to up her game tremendously going forward.

Trust Check

Getting real with an employee and putting radical candor into practice can be daunting. Those difficult conversations, as a manager or as an employee on the receiving end, can involve discussing "ums" in presentations or far more serious issues. However, if the straightforward truth is employed using the best of intentions to support and build up rather than tear down an employee, it builds a strong foundation of trust.

It's about caring for your employees. A key element of the exchange between Sandberg and Scott was trust. Sandberg had regularly demonstrated that she truly cared about Scott (and their entire team) and that she wanted the best for her, so there was already an established trust when Sandberg pulled Scott aside.

If you are lucky enough to have a boss or a colleague who cares — who is willing to let you know how you can improve your performance with straightforwardness, honesty, and positive intentions — it can help you grow professionally, as well as personally, even though it may be hard to hear at the moment.

Caring Personally

The caring-personally aspect of Scott's radical candor method is especially important. She stresses that it's important to go beyond just being professional and advocates bringing your whole self to the job, something she refers to as the "give a damn" axis. Scott observes that, early on, we're told we need to be professional at work, and somehow being professional has come to mean the need to, as Scott describes, "... leave your emotions ... leave your humanity... leave the very best part of yourself at home." Bringing your whole self to the job includes giving a damn and caring personally. You are never going to do the best work of your life if you leave half of yourself at home.

Challenge Directly

The challenging-directly aspect of the radical candor method Scott refers to as the "willing to piss people off" axis. Scott points out that a key part of being a good leader is being willing to say things that are difficult to hear — things that could make a person feel uncomfortable or upset. You must be willing to say what you really think. This creates the opportunity for either your thinking to be corrected or your employee's thinking to be corrected. If your employee's thinking needs a shift, then it's time to get real and not beat around the bush to address a tough topic.

Sweet Spot

The aim, according to Scott, is to move as high up on the "caring personally/challenge directly" axes as possible to land in radical candor territory. This sweet spot helps to avoid aggression, inauthentic empathy, and manipulation and creates a space with genuine compassion with room for developmental growth.

I've long been a proponent of straightforward feedback at work — doing my best to be constructively frank with those who reported to me and looking for that same frankness from those to whom I've reported. The radical candor approach involves asking, "How can I help my employees be the best versions of themselves?" "How can I best let them know how they can improve and move to the next level?" "What do they have to share in response?"

There's no question that vulnerabilities can bubble to the surface when radical candor is at play, but addressing issues early on is better than letting them go unchecked — which can lead to far greater pain and misunderstanding.

The radical candor I've received over the years has helped me to become a better listener. It has pushed me out of my comfort zone, helped me aim for higher goals, and helped me lead with humility and self-confidence. Radical candor is an opportunity to share two-way feedback in a spirit of good faith and growth. It's truth to power in a space of psychological safety.

Scott sees radical candor as a moral obligation to share the truth as you see it — to challenge and be challenged in return. While there's no denying the truth can hurt, the truth can also set both the manager and employee free in terms of improved trust and communication, helping to foster far greater success in the long run.

I encourage you to give and receive radically candid feedback in the spirit of helping others thrive and becoming the best version of yourself. It will change the way you navigate your life and career.

PRO TIPS

- Radical candor can improve your performance with straightforwardness, honesty, and positive intentions and help you grow, even though it may be hard to hear in the moment.

- As a leader, you have an obligation to share the truth — to challenge and be challenged in return.

- The truth can set the manager and employee free in terms of improved trust and communication, helping to foster greater success in the long run.

- Practice radical candor and encourage your direct reports and colleagues to do the same to create a culture of continuous growth and development.

CHAPTER 17

HONE YOUR GRIT AND RESILIENCE

Grit is firmness of spirit or mind. It's demonstrating unyielding courage in the face of challenge or danger. Since the career world is changing so fast, grit has become a sought-after competency and a necessity for entrepreneurs and innovators.

Research indicates that grit can determine success or achievement far more accurately than grades, credentials, or professional pedigree. Linda Kaplan Thaler and Robin Koval take a close look at why grit matters in their bestseller *Grit to Great: How Perseverance, Passion, and Pluck Take You from Ordinary to Extraordinary.*[16] I met them after hearing them speak at an event about why grit matters and how it can empower you in life and your career.

Grit to Great

Kaplan Thaler and Koval write about how the whole self-esteem movement has been a flop. Giving every kid a trophy merely for participating in a game has created a culture of mediocrity and lackluster achievement, undermining the natural grit that this nation of immigrants has relied on in order to build a new life in a new land.

Outstanding accomplishments aren't achieved just by showing up. They're the result of an individual's relentless commitment, courage, and stamina to overcome obstacles, which blows mediocrity out of the water. Luckily, one of the best things about grit is that you need not be born with it.

Grit can be developed.

Here are some action steps to hone your personal grit and move you from good to great. The GRIT steps of Guts, Resilience, Initiative, and Tenacity are inspired by Kaplan Thaler and Koval.

Guts – It all begins with the courage to take on new and tough challenges. Once you have that mindset, it's a matter of honing your confidence and taking a calculated risk. When things get tough or uncertain, you don't waver in the face of adversity. It's about being daring without being reckless and declaring your intention to triumph, even when it appears daunting.

Resilience – Failure happens, but gritty people know how to recover from failure and become stronger. It's called elasticity. This is what makes you follow an opportunity down an unknown path, and it's also your ability to re-route and pivot when the unexpected happens so you can achieve the end goal.

Initiative – Leaders are often judged by their ability to take the initiative and make things happen. Skill merged with action leads to achievement. Don't get stuck in the dream or ideation phase. Start doing something that will take you toward the end goal — now. Many people get stuck in the visioning phase and don't activate the plan to move forward.

Tenacity – Be relentless about staying focused on the goal. While the route to the goal will likely change, being industrious and determined is essential and will keep you moving forward. Great accomplishments take time. Malcolm Gladwell's research indicates that it takes about 10,000 hours to become an expert in anything from playing the violin to investment banking. Overnight success is rarely achieved, and the tenacious are prepared for the long and winding road.

Be Open to Plans B, C, D, and Beyond

While the end goal may stay consistent (or not), there will undoubtedly be twists and turns on the journey to attaining it. Gritty professionals adapt. They're flexible and willing to change course if it helps them move toward the goal. Kaplan Thaler and Koval tell a great story about the iconic movie *Jaws*. During filming, Plan A was to feature the ferocious shark prominently throughout the film, with a giant mechanical beast poised to scare the daylights out of each audience member.

Unfortunately, the mechanical shark proved to be extremely problematic during the filming, and the film was also over budget and past schedule. As the director, Steven Spielberg had to adapt and change course. His Plan B relied on music. He decided to suggest the shark's presence with the ominous and minimalistic theme music created by the composer John Williams. Think back to how seldom the shark is seen on-screen. The anticipatory effect of the music is brilliant — viewers didn't actually have to see the shark to feel the terror of its presence. Now considered one of the greatest films ever made, Spielberg's gritty resourcefulness, tenacity, and initiative have kept *Jaws* in the film spotlight for 40-plus years.

Bend Like Bamboo

Bamboo is one of the strongest plants because its hollow stem gives it the flexibility to bend in wind and weather. Its high compressive strength makes it stronger than brick, wood, or concrete, and its tensile strength is like steel.

Bamboo is gritty, and you can be, too. Here are some grit builders for you to put into practice:

- **Become an over-preparer** – Practice, prepare, and think of all the angles, so you are ready for the unexpected.

- **Get the gig** – Leverage your strengths and muster your confidence to push yourself into exploring uncomfortable opportunities.

- **Go the extra thirty minutes** – Identify your most productive time of day and put in an extra 30 minutes during your unique and effective sweet-spot time.

- **Stop ideating and start doing** – Activate a plan and move it forward.

- **Get rejected. A lot**! – You grow from taking chances. You'll learn that when you get knocked down, you will survive. Rejection can be an impetus to work harder than you ever thought possible.

If developing your grit factor feels daunting, that's a good thing. Being gritty is not for everyone, and only you can determine if grit is in your future. Going from good to great requires a lot of hard work, but it can start with small and incremental changes.

PRO TIPS

- Grit is a firmness of mind or spirit that can be developed. It's an unyielding courage in the face of a challenge.

- Develop your elasticity to bend like bamboo, so you don't break when failure happens — because it will happen. Focus on your resiliency and celebrate how you recovered.

- Be prepared for your well-intentioned plans to change and be open to new possibilities.

- Take a chance by trying new things and taking risks to grow your grit. Rejection can be an impetus to work harder than you ever thought possible.

- Cultivate a bias to action and commit to doing one thing daily to move you toward your desired goal.

CHAPTER **18**

BE A HIGH ACHIEVER, NOT A WORKAHOLIC

It took me years to come to terms with the reality that I was a workaholic and that the schedule I was keeping was unhealthy and unsustainable. I was stuck in the work whirlwind and had convinced myself that I loved my work so much that it was okay to work around the clock. I was not being honest with myself. By working those long hours, I was missing my life.

High Achiever vs. Workaholic

Unhealthy organizations celebrate an addiction to overwork, but the tragic reality of workaholism is that it can also lead to burnout and serious illness. I walked that path and now know that suffering is optional. It's essential to shift perspectives. I've done this by focusing on being a high achiever instead of a workaholic. In this way, I still honor my strong work ethic, and I remain highly productive. But I also feel gratified and inspired by my work. I am not overwhelmed.

A high achiever differs from a workaholic in that they are results-driven and focus on the end goal. They use downtime to look ahead and prepare. Or they rest and rejuvenate instead of creating meaningless work to fill the time.

High achievers know when to turn up the intensity of their work. They give it their all and increase capacity only when the opportunity requires it, so they don't burn out from giving 110 percent all the time.

Stop the Busy Brag

Workaholics feed on being busy and often fill time and space with tasks that are not valuable or necessary. They are stuck in a mental block that makes them believe being busy equals important, and nothing is farther from the truth.

Some work cultures also encourage the busy brag, so fight the urge to wallow in how busy you are with fellow workaholics. Don't become a work martyr. Focus on how you are being strategic to work smarter and not harder so you can more fully enjoy your life and career.

Work Smarter

Research has shown that multitasking is not efficient or productive, as the human brain can only focus on one thing at a time. Singletasking allows you to focus fully on one thing. As a result, you're able to complete a task more quickly, which then allows you to move on to the next thing.

High achievers embrace singletasking and the clarity that comes with controlling your environment. For instance, instead of reacting to incoming email signals with a Pavlovian-like response, set aside a block of time dedicated only to answering emails.

High achievers are proactive in their work environment and design their day around the most important tasks — those that have the most significant return on investment of their precious time.

80 Percent Is Done

Savvy professionals embrace the "good enough to go" maxim birthed in the design-thinking paradigm of tech start-ups. Workaholics often get stuck in the perfectionism paradox and never let go of a project because they believe it can always be better.

High achievers believe that 80 percent complete can mean done when it moves the needle closer to the end goal. Tweaking and improvements can happen in the iteration and test-drive phases of a project. If the work product never sees the light of day because of workaholics who practice perfectionism, you might as well not have done the work at all.

Validation Seekers

Workaholics often want to be seen as overachiever workhorses who put in long hours and burn the midnight oil. They buy into the overworking culture and consider it a badge of honor that should be celebrated.

If your car is in the company parking lot late at night and every weekend or your home office computer is on all hours of the night, then you are a work martyr, not a high achiever. Leaders must model behaviors that establish a high-achieving work culture that honors vacation time, work-life integration, sustainable hours, and flexibility that promotes mental and physical wellness. This is the kind of work environment that develops and nurtures high-achiever talent.

If you need validation, seek it out and ask for constructive feedback. Don't assume the unsustainable cycle of being the last one in the office will earn you the recognition you are seeking.

Honor Your Play Time

High achievers value life outside of work as much as their careers. They focus on sustainable practices that include a wellness regimen and playtime. Think about how you played as a child with reckless abandon and no set agenda.

Career-focused grown-ups especially need playtime to allow fun to be a significant part of their life. Playtime has measurable benefits that include boosting your creativity and giving your brain a chance to reboot, both of which lead to productivity.

When was the last time you gave yourself permission to play and do something that was laugh-out-loud fun?

Steps Toward Recovery

Moving from workaholism to being a high achiever requires a conscious effort. For me, workaholism was an addiction. Like any unhealthy behavior, it took time to learn and sustain healthy habits for the long run. And it took serious reprogramming before I was able to truly make the switch.

Here are some action steps to help you get started on a healthier work path.

- **Don't skimp on rest**. Each night, get the amount of sleep your body needs to function well. Don't compromise on this. If you are overtired and run down, you're more likely to get sick, and the recuperation time will result in you being even further behind.

- **Set clear boundaries.** If you are the only one who stays late, works in the evenings, and is there on weekends, something is wrong. Set boundaries and stick to them.

- **Eat real food.** Eat whole foods — things like fruits, vegetables, whole grains, and proteins that are not processed and preservative-laden. Take the time to prepare your lunch and bring it with you so you have control over what you're eating when things get crazy at work (and don't raid the vending machine). Take a break and eat your food slowly so you taste every bite. If you eat food quickly, you are more likely to overeat and gain weight. Back away from the computer and enjoy your well-earned lunch break.

- **Make time for friends and loved ones.** Be present with your family and make time for those you love. Work is important, but so is family, so be *in the moment* when you are with them. Spend quality time enjoying your loved ones and not thinking about work.

135

- **Get out into nature.** Take a walk outside to stretch your legs and breathe some fresh air during your workday. A short break can help you regroup, refresh, and let the stress roll off your shoulders.

- **Step away from the computer at home.** Avoid the urge to constantly check your work messages at home. Unplug from work and the technology that tethers you to it every now and then so you can enjoy some peaceful time at home. Create deal-breaker boundaries and share them with colleagues so you teach people how to treat you.

- **Evaluate your life purpose.** Reflect on what you are doing that is creating an imbalance in your life and really think about your personal goals. Consider your behavior and your health. Ask yourself if you are truly happy and fulfilled. If you answer yes, then you may be okay with your current sense of balance, but if you are unhappy, remember that you are in control of making a change for the better.

In addition to these steps, I also recommend that you consider an accountability partner you can turn to for support to help you reprogram your habits and commit to this new life plan.

High achievers do extraordinary work while also enjoying their lives. While the temptation is always there for me to slip back into my workaholic habits and unsustainable behaviors, I've learned to recognize when that happens and work to get myself back on track. What's helpful is that the life of a high achiever is so much more compelling and gratifying. I highly recommend giving it a try.

PRO TIPS

- Reflect on whether you are currently a workaholic and what might be missing in your life.

- Honor your mental and physical wellness needs and listen to what your body needs to honor your well-being.

- Consider whether you are working in an organization that expects and celebrates work addiction and if this is the place where you can thrive as a high achiever.

- Give yourself permission to become a high achiever and ditch being a work martyr.

- Find an accountability partner to help you focus on small, incremental steps to change your work habits to let your life back into your focus.

Pay-It-Forward Opportunity

You've made it halfway through the book, and I hope the resources and action steps are helping you navigate your career challenges and celebrate your incredible accomplishments. In the spirit of paying it forward, if you believe the book is providing value for you, I ask you to consider taking 60 seconds to leave a brief review of *Your Career Advantage* on Amazon.

I'm on a mission to empower individuals to thrive in both their life and career. Your review will help others in need find my book, so they can begin to make positive steps toward their own happier and healthier work lives. I have benefitted from the coaching and wisdom of others, and I want to continue to pay it forward to impact positive change for those who need it most.

Thank you for considering this free goodwill opportunity and for supporting me in my quest to make the world of work a better place. Enjoy the rest of the book!

WELL-BEING AT WORK

*How to Excel in Your Career
and Honor Your Health*

CHAPTER **19**

DON'T BE A CAREER LOSER

Depression, anxiety, stress, and overwhelm are at an all-time global high. That's a message to every one of us. We need to get serious about taking care of ourselves and living a healthy life. The benefits of making healthy choices are endless and have a positive impact on your work life as well — improving productivity, decreasing burnout, and more. In this chapter, I'll provide actionable tips detailing how you can honor your mind, body, and spirit so you can do your best work and live your best life.

Workaholism Is the Only Addiction We Celebrate!

There is a cultural misconception that you must be a workaholic to achieve high performance levels, but that's simply not true. In fact, there are many healthy choices you can make at work that won't sacrifice your professional values, relationships, or the expertise you provide to your organization. It's time to make these choices because workaholism is not sustainable and doesn't ensure productivity or happiness.

I've organized workers into two categories — high achievers and workaholics. Because both of these groups work hard, they may look the same on the outside. But there's a big difference in how these individuals feel on the inside and how they relate to their work.

A high achiever works hard in healthy, sustainable ways and feels happy and inspired.

A workaholic works hard in unhealthy, unsustainable ways and feels unhappy and burned out.

You have a choice. I gradually made the switch from workaholic to high achiever. And I forgive myself for any occasional backsliding since changing a behavior is an ongoing journey.

Take Time to Recharge

My life often resembles a roller coaster with ups and downs of activity — never a consistent, steady balance. And that's okay. The fact that I am aware of this is the key to keeping the imbalance at bay. I conduct periodic reality checks to help me navigate ultra-busy career times and then offset them with precious downtime when I can recharge.

I'll admit that for many years while working in several different organizations, I did not take the time I needed to recharge.

142

The biggest proof of my neglect is that I didn't take all of my accrued vacation time. Shame on me! This is not a badge of honor. It's the badge of a self-proclaimed PTO loser who gave away precious time earned as part of a compensation package.

Sadly, I'm not alone. Most adults are overworked and overwhelmed. But the counterintuitive reality is that they are not taking all the paid time off they've earned.

For years, we have been asked to do more with less, and workers are overstretched, stressed out, and exhausted. The always-on, 24/7 work culture is taking a heavy toll and resulting in millions of wasted vacation days. But skipping time off doesn't produce the outcome people expect. They don't "catch up" on accumulating work.

Instead, forfeiting time away undermines personal and economic well-being and, more importantly, mental and physical health. Taking earned time off is essential not only for a productive workforce but also for strong bonds with family and friends and a fulfilled life. In fact, there is research that shows taking time off will help you be more productive and healthy in life and your career.

Make It a Habit

In addition to taking time off, it's important to incorporate smaller recharge moments throughout your week. Many global work cultures celebrate wellness with days off to focus on health and well-being. Americans need to catch up on this proactive investment in health. From wellness practices to a hike in the woods or simple downtime to catch up on your favorite nonwork-related reading — do something just for you on a regular basis and reap the health benefits.

A nonweekend day of rest can also do wonders to help your body relax and rejuvenate.

Be the Leader Who Sets a Good Example

The debilitating culture of overwork will be changed by those who set a good example, and I hope you'll become a positive role model. If you manage others in your work environment, understand that your behavior sets an example for your colleagues. If you honor your vacation time, your coworkers will follow suit and take what's owed to them without guilt or concern.

Lead by example and truly unplug during your time away.

 A vacation should not just be a change of scenery, so you can do your work in a different location.

Benefits of Time Away

Time away from work impacts you holistically. Consider the effect it can have on your personal and work life:

Mental Health – Getting out of the race can reduce the pressure you're feeling and give your emotions a chance to reboot and relax.

Cognitive Health – Taking a breath and reducing your focus on work gives you the distance needed to gain a better perspective and think more clearly.

Social Well-Being – Allowing yourself to be fully present with family and loved ones is not only good for you, but it's also good for your work colleagues. It shows your colleagues you trust them and demonstrates that you don't need to be tethered to them during your time away.

Development and Empowerment – Letting coworkers take the reins helps you *and* them. When the boss is away, others get the chance to step up, take responsibility, and cover essential tasks, which provides professional development, learning, and growth opportunities. This benefits the whole team in the long run.

Organizational Calm – Providing clarity about the chain of command during your absence helps. Work with your team to create procedures that prevent bottlenecks so systems run smoothly to prevent unnecessary stress and ambiguity for others while you are away.

Heart Health – Taking a break from work is meant to be relaxing. In fact, the American Psychological Association's annual Work and Well-being survey and report conclude that time away from work reduces stress by removing people from activities and environments that are the source of stress.[17] The potential cardiovascular health benefits of taking a vacation include reduced risk of heart disease, lower blood pressure, decreased depression, and less stress.

Plan Ahead

Leading by example and modeling the way are great ways to show others the importance of taking time off. By truly detaching from work and taking the time to recharge, you let your team know they can, too.

Instead of being a work martyr, look ahead and consider how you can utilize your precious PTO over the next 12 months. Block off days on your calendar now for wellness breaks as well as longer chunks of time for vacations. Don't be a vacation loser and let this well-earned benefit go unused. Paid time off is precious and was put in place to help you live a healthier life. It's up to you to take advantage of this resource and honor yourself in the process.

PRO TIPS

- Paid time off is part of your organization's benefits package —don't leave your hard-earned money on the table.

- Switch from workaholic behavior to being a high achiever.

- Reap the mental, physical, and emotional health benefits of unplugging from work.

- Acknowledge that time away from work sets a good example for others.

- Plan your full PTO allotment in advance for the next calendar year to ensure you use it all.

CHAPTER **20**

THE GIFT OF
PLAY AND SLEEP

Consider the gifts of play and rest to honor what your immune system and body need to thrive.

I always knew sleep was essential for health and well-being. But I didn't always follow the sleep advice of health experts. I see so many people caught up in the myth that hard-working and successful people must sacrifice this important aspect of their life for their careers. That is a dangerous roller coaster to be on, and it's a constant reminder that we all must set personal boundaries.

Working long hours doesn't translate into productivity, and the false badge of honor people wear for being sleep-deprived and overworked is extremely unhealthy and unsustainable, not to mention unnecessary.

Refocus and place emphasis on productivity and not on the number of hours you toil at work. I'm reminded of *The*

Sleep Revolution author Arianna Huffington's savvy words: "If success looks like overwork, constant stress, and sleeplessness — I don't want it!" [18]

The lesson is simple and implementable. Design a unique life that replenishes your energy and honors your body.

Sleep is Nonnegotiable

Getting a good night's sleep has many benefits you may not have considered. It can lead to:

- **A stronger immune system**
- **Weight loss**
- **Better sex**
- **Clarity of mind**

Every adult should get between seven and nine hours of sleep each night. However, you alone can determine the number of sleep hours that are best for you. Of course, there are occasions when the baby gets up in the middle of the night, your partner's snoring keeps you awake, or your geriatric dog needs to be let outside. Life happens! But it's important to strive to be more in control of your sleep on a regular basis. Create a bedtime ritual and sleep schedule that permits you to focus on your sleep every night, so when the occasional sleep disturbances happen, their effects are minimal.

Bedtime Ritual

The nightly preparation of going to bed signals to your body that it's time to relax and rejuvenate after a long day. Here are some tips to consider when creating your own evening plan:

- Wear specific bedclothes (pajamas, nightshirt, etc.) and not garments you wear during the day.
- Put your digital devices to bed — outside of your bedroom and out of eyesight and earshot. A digital detox is essential for peaceful sleep.
- Eliminate alcohol, caffeine, and digital screens a few hours prior to bedtime to give your brain and body time to prepare for sleep.
- Choose an alarm clock with a soothing tone to awaken you gently — not one that will frighten you awake with a startling noise.

Don't Sacrifice Sleep for Work

Sleep deprivation is dangerous, and those who constantly burn the midnight oil without resting deplete their bodies of the energy needed to restore and heal each day. Sleep nurtures the brain, and prolonged lack of sleep is like alcohol or drug use — impairing motor skill functions and mental clarity.

We know that driving while drunk is dangerous and unlawful, yet millions go to work sleep-deprived (many driving there). This sleep deprivation parallels an intoxicated state, with symptoms including a lack of clarity and poor judgment. Remember that the most important thing we bring to work is our judgment.

Respect your body with rest. Over 70 percent of stress-related health conditions can be reduced or eliminated with proper sleep. What matters is your energy and focus, not the amount of time you put into things. Consider how you can work smarter, not longer, to be more productive in life and your career.

Make Time to Play

How much time do you devote to play in your life? Think of play as something that brings you pure joy. Disqualify competitive sports or working out if there is a goal attached, like winning a game or losing weight, etc. These activities should bring you great happiness and pleasure without stress or an end goal.

Perhaps you find joy in hiking with your dog in the woods or cooking a special meal for loved ones. Think about how you currently make room for joy in your life (or don't!), and consider how you can design a life with more joyful opportunities.

Joy, the state of elation, happiness, and delight, is a natural stress reliever. By making more time for play in your life, you will reduce your stress level and create space for happiness.

Reset Your Intention with Work and Life Priorities

There seems to be a major shift occurring in the world of work and life. People are starting to realize that the myth of burning the candle at both ends to achieve success and promotion is not worth perpetuating. They feel burning out should not be the price for achieving success. In fact, it shouldn't be a trade-off between living a well-rounded life and reaching high-performance levels because work performance is improved when you prioritize your health and well-being. Making room for rest and joy in life leads to a healthier populace, improves work productivity, and results in a less stressful integration of life and career.

Consider how you can embody the importance of balancing work and life by being a role model in your place of work. You can set an example and create a culture with a strong work ethic — a culture that leads to wellness and does not sacrifice play and rest. Modeling a workplace that values making time for the things that matter in life outside of work will lead to recruiting and retaining talent of all ages in organizations.

Honor the Only Body You Have

I will always be ambitious, focused, determined, and goal-oriented, but I now understand that if I honor my body with sleep and try to mitigate stress, my body will honor me back with wellness of mind and spirit. The biggest shift for me was embracing the concept of relinquishing control. Arianna Huffington says, "Life is a dance between making it happen and letting it happen." I, for one, am trying to move from struggle to release.

I'm learning to be less concerned with working longer hours and instead focus on being efficient and more strategic with my time. Additionally, I'm intentional about sleep and play, which adds more joy to my life. I feel refreshed, energized, and nurtured when I optimize both my play and work time.

PRO TIPS

- Overworking is not a badge of honor.

- Prioritize playtime to create space for joy.

- Sleep is nonnegotiable for a healthy life and career.

- Create a bedtime ritual that includes a digital detox from devices.

- Reset your intentions and honor the body you have so it can serve you well.

CHAPTER 21

EMPLOYEE LANGUISHING – IT'S A THING

Let's be real — there is a lot happening in the world. I'm a glass-half-full person. Positivity is one of my top ten CliftonStrengths themes. However, I do believe the weight of the world is impacting how we navigate our daily lives, and some days just feel *meh*.

By definition, *meh* means expressing a lack of interest or enthusiasm. Meh even has an emoji. Many people experiencing meh are assessing their career lives to determine whether their values are being met or not. Prolonged meh can morph into languishing and be a risk factor for depression. It's the absence of well-being. As Adam Grant, Wharton School professor and organizational psychologist, says in his TED Talk, "It's as if everything in life is in grayscale as opposed to vivid color — the sense of being a little joyless or aimless. While someone who we say is flourishing has a powerful sense of meaning and mastery, languishing can dull motivation and interfere with our focus...."[19]

Organizations can't ignore this trend and need to develop proactive strategies to help their employees avoid meh and encourage them to flourish.

How Organizations Can Be Proactive

While finding your mojo is an individual experience, according to Grant, leaders in organizations can also take steps to address employee languishing. The following strategies can help you help your team.

1. **Broaden your understanding of mental health and well-being.** Learn about the impact of mental health challenges and develop programs and resources that help people holistically.

2. **Take a preventative, more holistic approach.** Prevention costs far less than crisis management. And it leads to higher performing and more engaged employees, which improves retention.

3. **Leadership must model behaviors that drive lasting change.** Create space for psychological safety where all can be authentic without fear of negative consequences. Share your own ideas freely to demonstrate that you believe personal risk-taking is safe within the team. Build an environment where team members feel accepted and respected.

4. **Use coaching to help employees build key mindsets and behaviors.** Offering coaching resources can be one of the best ways to help employees develop resilience and practice self-compassion.

Culture of Care

I heard Jason Lippert, president and CEO of LCI Industries, speak at an event. His company is a great example of a workplace that incorporates all the strategies mentioned above. He talked about how he and his team initiated a cultural transformation by finding creative ways to develop leadership and improve corporate culture. LCI's initiative is known as *Everyone Matters,* and Lippert's philosophy states, "By caring for others more genuinely while at work, you develop trusting relationships. Your team members become like family, and family tends to stick together." [20]

Lippert hired a team of leadership directors who spend time coaching and working on personal and professional development with company leaders. The company's *Lippert Dream Achiever Program* provides personal development coaches for frontline team members as well. This program provides a safe space where employees can talk about life challenges and obtain guidance in creating personal and professional goals. Employee retention at the company is exceptional, and the business is thriving, so the return on investment of Lippert's initiative is clear.

The fact that development coaches are a significant element of the program underscores the value that coaching can provide for employees at every level. As a coach, this warms my heart!

Find Your Flow

The best predictor of well-being in the workplace is flow, which is a feeling of being in the zone or totally absorbed in an activity. I think of it as someone's happy place where they totally lose track of time. Peak flow requires you to be actively doing something you truly enjoy.

To find your flow, get started on a project that challenges and interests you. Find your momentum with small wins. It's also important to truly focus on a single task. Flow requires this boundary so you can dedicate your full attention to something you enjoy doing. Think about what matters to you when finding your flow. Who is impacted by your work? Dig deep to see the faces, know their names, and consider how you are impacting others.

Flow can be a team experience as well. If you are a leader of people, honor your team's well-being and give them the tools to find their flow. When your team is in flow, they experience heightened focus, productivity, and happiness engaging in the work together.

In a world where languishing is real, we must all be accountable for the well-being of our teams and ourselves. Since languishing can also be a tipping point into burnout, leaders and organizations must be mindful of creating work environments that nurture well-being. It's okay to have bad days — nobody likes the toxic positivity of a person who is artificially perky all the time. Instead, honor your emotions and consider how you can bring more color into the grayscale of languishing or *meh* and move toward motivation and flow.

"Peak moments of flow are having fun with the people we love."
— **Adam Grant** from his TED Talk on "How to Stop Languishing and Start Finding Flow"

PRO TIPS

- Organizations need proactive strategies that help their employees avoid meh and encourage them to flourish.

- Take a preventative and more holistic approach to well-being.

- Create a culture of caring in your workplace.

- Engage professional coaches to empower individuals to become the best version of themselves in a confidential and supportive space.

- Leaders must model behaviors for lasting change.

- The best predictor of well-being is flow — know how to find it.

CHAPTER **22**

THE BURNOUT SURPRISE

Not a day goes by that I don't encounter someone experiencing burnout. It's real, it's intense, and it's debilitating. Most equate physical exhaustion and prolonged stress with a lack of self-care. While burnout does have physical manifestations, the root cause is something more and will be a revelation. I spoke to Paula Davis, CEO of The Stress and Resilience Institute, about her book, *Beating Burnout at Work: Why Teams Hold the Secret to Well-Being & Resilience,* on my *Your Working Life* podcast. [21]

In the book, she shares her candid experience of burning out during her last year of practicing law. At the time, she thought she needed to ramp up her self-care to fix it. But after a decade of research and study on burnout, Davis believes that to fix the problem, we need to address the underlying causes.

"You can't yoga your way out of burnout." – **Paula Davis**

Burnout

To begin, we need to understand what burnout is and how it impacts us. It's more than just being exhausted or stressed out. In a *Forbes* article, Davis identifies the three primary aspects of burnout: [22]

- **Burnout is not an interchangeable word with general stress.** Stress exists on a continuum and becomes something more like burnout when you experience chronic exhaustion, cynicism, inefficacy, or lost impact. The term burnout is often used too loosely or in the wrong context to describe a general tiredness or what people often just call having a bad day. It's neither of those things.

- **Burnout is a workplace issue.** Davis defines burnout as the manifestation of chronic workplace stress, and the World Health Organization's definition of the term makes clear that "burnout refers specifically to phenomena in the occupational context and should not be applied to describe experiences in other areas of life."[23]

- **Burnout is complex.** People oversimplify burnout when they only focus on one of the big symptoms of it — exhaustion — and prescribe self-help remedies like more sleep, time management techniques, or exercise as quick fixes. This misses the bigger factors driving burnout that are found in your workplace environment, like how your boss leads, the quality of your team, and even macro-level issues (i.e., changing industry regulations that shift organizational priorities, which influences how leaders lead their teams and impacts how frontline workers work).

To decrease burnout, organizations need to identify and deal with the causes and create organization-wide solutions. **Burnout happens when there is an imbalance between job demands and job resources.**

Christina Maslach from the University of California, Berkeley, has identified six core work demands that organizations, leaders, and teams need to address in order to decrease the likelihood of burnout.[24]

1. **Lack of autonomy** – Having no choice as to how and when you perform the tasks related to your work.

2. **High workload and work pressure** – Particularly problematic in combination with too few resources.

3. **Lack of leader/colleague support** – Not feeling a sense of belonging at work.

4. **Unfairness** – Favoritism; arbitrary decision-making.

5. **Value disconnect** – What you find important about work doesn't match the environment you're in.

6. **Lack of recognition** – No feedback; you rarely, if ever, hear thank you.

Organizational Issues Can't Be Fixed with a Wellness App

Understanding that burnout is a workplace issue was an epiphany for me. It shed so much light on the systemic cause of burnout. As a leader with direct reports, it also inspired me to be more conscious of what my colleagues really needed to thrive in their lives and careers.

On my podcast, Paula Davis suggests ways to build a positive culture at work and stresses the importance of being consistent. One of the easiest and best ways to do this is by deploying what she calls TNTs — tiny noticeable things. Leaders can take these small, consistent actions to create a positive culture and avoid employee burnout.

Here are ten easy-to-implement TNTs that make a difference.

- Say thank you more (probably much more) than you currently do.
- Offer in-time feedback to peers and direct reports.
- Be clear when giving assignments and talk with other senior leaders to minimize conflicting requests and ambiguity (two known accelerants of burnout).
- Make constructive feedback a learning-focused, two-way conversation.
- Keep people informed of changes.
- Keep track of and talk about small wins and successes.
- Encourage team members.
- Provide a rationale or explanation for projects, goals, and big-picture vision.
- Clarify confusing and missing information related to roles and tasks.

- Prioritize "you matter" cues, like calling people by name, making eye contact, and giving colleagues your full attention.

Reframing Self-Care

I'll always be an advocate for self-care, but I now see that it is not a burnout cure. Burnout is an organizational and cultural issue that everyone in an organization needs to address. Using the strategies discussed in this chapter, you can cultivate a workplace environment where employees thrive rather than burn out.

PRO TIPS

- Organizations must seek the root cause of burnout and apply systemic remedies.

- Consider values, recognition, resources, and autonomy when mitigating burnout causes in an organization.

- Broaden your view of self-care and include how you engage and interact with coworkers to create a positive environment.

- Focus on the tiny, noticeable things that can leave a lasting impact on workplace culture.

CHAPTER 23

REST IS MORE THAN SLEEP

I thought I was honoring my need to rest, but my mind was blown when I learned about Dr. Saundra Dalton-Smith and delved into the nuances of rest beyond sleep and why we need to change our perspective about how we recharge.

Dr. Saundra Dalton-Smith is a board-certified internal medicine physician, work-life integration researcher, and author of the bestselling book *Sacred Rest: Recover Your Life, Renew Your Energy, Restore Your Sanity.*[25]

She shows high achievers how to optimize their time and effort without sacrificing their happiness and relationships, both personally and professionally. The good doctor had me hooked at *high achiever* since I struggle on the slippery slope of workaholism and the quest for work-life balance.

After devouring her book, I invited Dr. Saundra Dalton-Smith to join me for an episode of my podcast,

Your Working Life. I learned a lot from her, which I am on a mission to share.

Rest Is Not Just About Sleep

If you're feeling tired or worn out, you may feel like you just need to get more sleep. While sleep is important, rest is about more than how many hours you're asleep. Dr. Dalton-Smith describes it as follows:

> So many people count rest as a big bucket. A cessation of activity. Anything that is not their normal work, they call rest. You'll hear from someone, 'I'm going on vacation to rest.' What they really mean is that they are going to go to a fun location and do fun work. They're not effectively resting — they're doing a lot of fun activities that usually don't leave them feeling restored but rather leave them feeling more tired when they get home.

Let's not forget that some people (and I have been guilty of this!) have trouble severing the tether from work and are simply working from another location while on vacation. So, rest is not truly happening.

This raises the question of whether you can really be productive while burning the candle at both ends. According to Dr. Saundra Dalton-Smith:

> ... the most productive people — people who produce at the highest mental, physical, creative,

emotional level of capacity — rest. Those people cannot do that unless they are getting adequate rest. Otherwise, you are creating and producing out of emptiness.

There are a lot of people in the world who are producing work but the work they're producing is not their best. Whether you're a creative, a writer, an actor, an entrepreneur, a schoolteacher, a student, whatever, if you're trying to get to the next level, you won't get there empty. You're only going to get there when you feel at your best — fully empowered and fully energized.

Resist the Sleep Deprivation Celebration

Many organizations and leaders perpetuate a false badge of honor for working around the clock and getting by on very little sleep. I once had a boss who told me, "I'll sleep when I'm dead." Enough said.

Dr. Dalton-Smith believes we need to be courageous and defy the status quo. Approach your rest needs on an individual basis and honor your mind and body. This is not a competition or a comparison — you, alone, are in control of your wellness. Tap into your inner rebel and blaze your own path. As Dr. Dalton-Smith says, "It takes courage because that [prioritizing rest] is not what most of the world is doing, and that is why most of the world is burned out, tired, and fatigued."

Seven Types of Rest

In her book *Sacred Rest*, Dr. Dalton-Smith identifies the seven specific types of rest we need to feel happy, productive, and fulfilled. She identified these categories as essential when diagnosing common ailments in her patients. She realized that helping her patients get these seven types of rest often restored their health. Some of these may surprise you.

1. **Mental Rest** – When your mind is tired, your memory lapses, and you are prone to making mistakes. Your mental monkey chatter of self-criticisms and thoughts about what you "would-a, could-a, should-a" wears out your brain. It's important to balance this out by scheduling activities throughout the day that ground you and take little thought. Take a walk outside and breathe the fresh air. Sit still and meditate for a few moments to give your brain a chance to reboot.

2. **Spiritual Rest** – Consider your life's purpose and your connection to something bigger than yourself. Bask in the sunlight or enjoy the scent of flowers in bloom. Take a moment to listen to the rain or share your gratitude about something awesome.

3. **Emotional Rest** – The constant pressure to perform at work or at home can lead to overwhelm. Identify a circle of people you trust and create a space of psychological safety where you can let down your guard. Be vulnerable and share your full range of emotions with them — from fear to joy and everything in between.

4. **Social Rest** - In-person interactions are important. Find a community of like-minded people — a group you enjoy spending time with and who leave you feeling relaxed and happy after being together.

5. **Sensory Rest** - From screen time to loud noises, your senses can easily become overwhelmed beyond your control. Take a break from your devices, play your favorite music, and consider how to stimulate your olfactory senses with aromas you enjoy.

6. **Creative Rest** - Take the time to notice the details in things. Immerse yourself in something you enjoy — music, theatre, dance, comedy, sports — something that will re-awaken your curiosity. Go back to a beginner's mindset and experience something with a fresh, new perspective to tap your creative juices.

7. **Physical Rest** - Your body needs recovery time. Many professionals sit in a chair for multiple hours each day. Even if you exercise regularly, honor your body by stretching and taking breaks to breathe deeply and reboot. This practice will calm your body and lift your mood.

Be brave and honor your rest needs holistically to help you recover your life and renew your energy. We must honor our body since it's the only one we have.

PRO TIPS

- Rest is not just about sleep.

- Be courageous and defy the status quo that burning the candle at both ends is a badge of honor.

- Consider honoring Dr. Saundra Dalton-Smith's seven types of rest: Mental, Spiritual, Emotional, Social, Sensory, Creative, and Physical.

- Honor what your mind and body need to produce your best work.

THE OFFICE VIBE

Company Culture Matters

CHAPTER 24

DESIGN YOUR WORKPLACE CULTURE

While ping pong tables and gourmet coffee bars may entice new recruits to work in a company, it's not enough to retain them long-term. Savvy leaders must learn how to design, live, and breathe a workplace culture that honors the people who work there. This section will help you roll up your sleeves and design a culture where everyone can do their best work.

There's an iconic quote from the late leadership guru Peter Drucker that states, "Culture eats strategy for breakfast." This is a visceral statement in an era when people are leaving companies in record numbers to seek work environments that honor their values and provide meaning and purpose. I had a great conversation with Melissa Daimler, chief learning officer for Udemy, on my *Your Working Life* podcast, where she shared actionable strategies to redesign workplace culture for lasting success.

Daimler's book, *ReCulturing: Design Your Company Culture to Connect with Strategy and Purpose for Lasting Success*, is a must-read for leaders serious about navigating the evolution of work and creating a desirable workplace culture.

Culture is What You DO, Not What You HAVE

Employees long to have a workplace culture that provides an environment and an experience where they can make an impactful contribution and stay in a career for the foreseeable future. Daimler posits, "ReCulturing is the continuous act of redesigning, reimagining, and reconnecting behaviors, processes, and practices to the organizational system." [26]

While the gourmet coffee bars and food trucks may be appealing to some employees in the short term, they are perks and do not reflect a company's purpose and strategy like culture should. Daimler is emphatic about culture being something we "do" and not something we "have."

Culture Is Not an HR Project

Most culture change initiatives fail because leaders view them as a one-and-done HR project. True culture change starts with letting go of what is not serving employees and the company well. It is a continuous process with no end. It's an ongoing co-creation that should involve employees and leaders and always be evolving.

Designing and evolving an organizational culture should be an all-play opportunity. When staff has buy-in with a strong culture, they enjoy where they work and are successful on an individual level, which scales to the success of the company at large.

Daimler says, "Culture is how work happens between people. It is every interaction that happens, every decision that is made — whether in-person or remotely. It is what we do — not what we have."

We must create a culture that exemplifies how we interact and treat each other at work. It's a behavioral playbook that promotes connection and engagement and illustrates how work happens between people.

Connect Strategy and Purpose to Culture

Referencing Drucker's quote about culture eating strategy for breakfast, Daimler quipped, "It's time culture and strategy eat breakfast together, maybe even lunch and the occasional dinner."

It's time to put company values into practice and create workplace environments where values are experienced throughout the lifecycle of an employee. At every stage, company culture needs to be communicated.

Hiring – Help prospective talent understand company values, behaviors, and culture during the interview process.

Onboarding – Create a sense of belonging that lasts by providing new employees with a thorough orientation process and training programs that immerse them into the behaviors of the company's culture.

Talent management and development – Create a learning lab environment where individuals can achieve mastery in key areas and have opportunities for ongoing professional development. This develops the company culture and builds a strong internal bench for succession planning and advancement opportunities.

Offboarding – Align employee departures with company values. You may not have considered how important culture, behaviors, and values are when offboarding an employee who is leaving your company. Savvy leaders know that employees who leave can continue to be positive brand ambassadors — or not. Stewarding relationships with alumni employees can lead to knowledge transfer, business development, and boomerang talent that returns with new and valuable experiences down the road. The way an employee exits your organization matters.

Continuous Culture Evolution

A commitment to "ReCulturing" takes the intentionality of leadership. It's not only about engagement surveys, which can be a great starting point. It is also about clarifying the company's values and communicating those values to employees.

Put simply, values are the beliefs your company stands for, and behaviors are the ways people act, individually and collectively. Words matter, so communicating those beliefs is important. To get started, it might be useful to think about the following:

- If you were to define three behaviors for each of your organizational values, what would they be?
- When you think about behaviors you see across your organization, which are foundational, core, and aspirational?

The creation of culture is as important as designing strategic plans. It's essential to define an organization's purpose. When the purpose is clear to employees, it inspires them and makes the work more meaningful, which translates into results. Purpose statements, like values, must bring people together and remind them of WHY they are doing the work of the organization.

Design a Culture to Empower People to Do Their Best Work

With the job market ripe with opportunities, people have options to work in organizations that practice a culture where they can thrive. Smart leaders will look at culture as an evolution and not a checklist item to finish. Continuous improvement is at the heart of a living culture, and leaders must be willing to listen regularly to what employees need and want in order to do their best work.

The world of work changed dramatically during the pandemic. To attract and retain top talent, culture is a must-have experience. Companies need to demonstrate actions and behaviors that are practiced and not just visible on the company website. Company culture will be a defining factor in the future of work and will distinguish successful companies over the long haul. If companies become learning organizations and commit to understanding what's working and where they need to develop, the results will be emotional agility and a company culture where people can thrive.

Daimler ended our podcast conversation by saying, "Culture is happening by design or default, so we might as well design our culture and be intentional about having what we want for our employees."

You have the power to impact the culture in your organization, and you deserve an organization with a culture where you can do your best work.

PRO TIPS

- Consider how culture connects behaviors, processes, and practices to the organizational system.

- To attract and retain top talent, know that culture is a must-have experience, demonstrated by actions and behaviors that are practiced.

- Focus on culture as something you "do," not something you "have."

- Be willing to listen regularly because continuous improvement is at the heart of a living culture.

CHAPTER **25**

PSYCHOLOGICAL SAFETY AT WORK

The term psychological safety is all the rage in workplace research and publications. It's important to demystify this term and break it down so it can be easily implemented in your work environment. If people feel safe to make mistakes, fail forward, or share differing viewpoints, great things happen. Cognitive diversity is fostered and celebrated, and productivity, innovation, and standards soar.

These savvy points from Katie Taylor provide a comprehensive look at psychological safety:[27]

- Psychologically safe work environments allow team members to feel they can safely take calculated risks without fear of repercussions.
- A lack of psychological safety may deter people from speaking up about mistakes, knowledge gaps, or potential problems.

- When working remotely, you can promote psychological safety by being intentional about scheduling one-on-one meetings, asking open-ended questions, modeling boundaries, and setting expectations for video meetings.

Workplace Behaviors

Amy C. Edmondson, a Novartis Professor of Leadership and Management at Harvard Business School, has extensively researched how organizations can create environments that provide psychological safety for employees.

Essentially, she organizes psychological safety into five workplace behaviors and describes what these behaviors look like in action.[28]

1. **Seeking or Giving Feedback** – Nurture an environment that encourages sharing positive and developmental feedback.

2. **Making Changes and Improvements** – Aways illustrate the WHY with workplace change, so colleagues understand their role in the change and how they can make an impact.

3. **Obtaining or Providing Help or Expertise** – Asking for help is a sign of intelligence and strength and not a sign of weakness. Be prepared to help or offer additional resources.

4. **Experimenting** – Adopt an iterative approach, like the design thinking process, where prototypes are tested and improved upon over time.

5. **Engaging in Constructive Conflict or Confrontation** – Address conflict quickly and don't let it fester. Minimize confrontation by leading with curiosity. Try responding with "Tell me more..." to diffuse the emotions and gain clarity.

Edmonson's iconic TED Talk, "How to Turn a Group of Strangers into a Team," is well worth watching. One of her key messages addresses the importance of psychological safety:

> Every time we withhold, we rob ourselves and our colleagues of small moments of learning, and we don't innovate. We don't come up with new ideas. We are so busy managing impressions that we don't contribute to creating a better organization.

Putting it Into Practice

These actionable steps can help you implement and nurture a work environment with psychological safety.

- **Approach conflict as a collaborator, not an adversary** – Work to create mutually desirable outcomes.
- **Speak human to human** – Recognize that everyone has beliefs, perspectives, opinions, anxieties, vulnerabilities, joys, and sorrows — it's part of the human condition.
- **Replace blame with curiosity** – Adopt a learning mindset, and don't assume you know all the facts; heighten your active listening and start by asking how you can support the other person.

- **Ask for feedback on delivery** – This creates a role model of humility and engenders trust. Receiving feedback (especially for leaders) shows a willingness to grow and develop.

Be Accountable

When was the last time you asked your team how safe they felt at work? This simple question can begin the conversation and then provide an opportunity for the team to work together to build a culture of psychological safety. It's not a one-and-done build. Creating team psychological safety takes time, buy-in, stewarding, and intentionality, but the results are worth the investment.

PRO TIPS

- Develop psychological safety, so team members feel they can safely take calculated risks without fear of repercussions.

- Teams and workplaces with psychological safety reap the benefits of cognitive diversity, productivity, innovation, and retention.

- Approach conflict as a collaborator, not an adversary; speak human to human; replace blame with curiosity; ask for feedback on delivery to build trust and engender psychological safety.

- Be accountable – psychological safety takes buy-in, stewarding, and intentionality, but the results are worth the investment.

CHAPTER 26

TIME TO THINK

The pandemic-generated work style of back-to-back meetings without transition time and overworked and overwhelmed employees has been dangerously normalized into the status quo. I hear from clients, friends, and colleagues that the daily meeting blitz leaves no time to do actual work. Evenings and weekends are spent catching up on the mountains of emails and projects that never got attention during the week.

Neuroscience and Work

What this constantly on-the-go state has shown us is that it's necessary to honor the resting state of your brain. While most organizations place value on doing things that focus solely on outcomes and results, the act of thinking, reflecting, and processing allows for higher insight and creativity.

It's important to give people space and time during the day to think and reflect. Companies like Google and 3M have incorporated this type of thinking time into the day. "Dabble time" is considered an important part of the workday, and employees report that these times have resulted in some of their most successful products.

Thinking time should be honored and prioritized, as it stimulates creativity and allows essential room to develop great work. The endless meeting cycle is counterproductive if process time is not part of the daily routine.

Thursday is the New Friday

Joe Sanok, author of *Thursday is the New Friday: How to Work Fewer Hours, Make More Money, and Spend Time Doing What You Want*, explains that we're stuck in an almost century-old model of work and productivity. The 40-hour workweek and eight-to-five work-day began in 1926 when Henry Ford first started assembly line auto manufacturing. Now, many of us work well over 40 hours a week, and the business day expands to accommodate our workload.[29]

I interviewed him on my *Your Working Life* podcast to find out more about how a four-day workweek works. Sanok's book is full of case studies about people and companies who have successfully embraced the less-is-more approach to work while meeting and exceeding goals and reinvigorating the human capital of employees. Throughout our discussion, he gave me some useful strategies that all of us can implement to improve productivity, including:

- Eliminate or reduce tasks (e.g., email, meetings, etc.) to make room for creative work and to mitigate stress, leading to more productive results.

- Slow down at work to be more productive, spark creativity, and improve focus.
- Experiment with a new schedule — find your sweet-spot work time (morning person or night owl?) and honor your brain by working when you are at your best, even if it's outside of traditional hours.
- Set and enforce daily, weekly, monthly, and annual boundaries to positively impact your personal and professional life.
- Let go of guilt as you design a healthier work life — give yourself permission to thrive.

White Space Allows for Your Best Work

Juliet Funt is a speaker, consultant, and self-proclaimed warrior in the battle against busyness. She has been in the trenches with thousands of busy people who tolerate the misery of work, and she has helped them exit the overwhelm paradigm to find satisfaction and enhanced productivity.

I interviewed Funt on my *Your Working Life* podcast about her book, *A Minute to Think: Reclaim Creativity, Conquer Busyness, and Do Your Best Work.* She talked about the power of space and time to think, breathe, reflect, and ponder to allow the spark of productivity to ignite. The missing element is what she calls white space — short periods of time that are open, unscheduled, and which, when recaptured, are able to change the very nature of work.

Funt says, "White space is the stepping back, the strategic pause, the oxygen that allows the sparks of our efforts to catch fire." [30] She believes that white space has the power to radically and simply reinvent the way we approach work in the maxed-out, continuous juggle of the work and life journey.

Liberate yourself from workload overwhelm:

- Schedule thinking time for yourself and your team to allow for questioning what's current and envisioning what's possible.
- Heart-centered leaders need to listen to find out what makes work miserable/challenging for direct reports and be open to the possibilities of creative solutions.
- Reclaim creativity by not overscheduling meetings — keep essential meetings to 45 minutes or less with an agenda.
- Eradicate the shame of rest at work — celebrate the power of reflection time.
- Delete unnecessary meetings from your schedule. Consider whether you really need to attend every meeting.
- Don't overuse the cc line in emails to avoid message overwhelm. Consider: *Whose Action is This?* and only cc those who are essential to the action.

It's time to challenge the way we have always worked. Innovative companies will retain top talent by recalibrating and empowering colleagues to do their best work with creative time and space to think, reflect, and process. If we slow down, we make room for more productive results and healthier employees.

Think of it as an experiment. Try incorporating some of these new practices for a few months and assess how it compares to what you've always done. You may find unexpected, innovative results you want to adopt long-term.

PRO TIPS

- The act of thinking, reflecting, and processing allows for higher insight and creativity.

- Schedule white space on your calendar to allow for focused time to think and reflect.

- Slow down at work to be more productive and spark creativity and focus.

- Experiment with something new for a few months, compare it to what you've always done, and then assess the results.

- Eradicate the shame of rest at work — celebrate the power of reflection time that enhances productivity in the long run.

CHAPTER 27

BEING BUSY IS NOTHING TO BRAG ABOUT

I conducted an informal social experiment and asked the question, "How are you?" to several individuals of different ages and career fields who live in various geographies and hold diverse perspectives. The people I queried all responded with some variation of how **busy** they were. Their responses were stress-filled and frustrated, and their self-reported state of being busy was clearly causing them angst.

Busyness is a dangerous trap. It's nearly impossible to find meaning and fulfillment in life when you are stuck in the quicksand of being busy. I am on a mission to disrupt the busyness culture and focus on a life that is measured by meaning, value, fulfillment, and other factors you can customize to celebrate your unique definition of happiness and satisfaction.

Busy Doesn't Mean Important

As a recovering workaholic, I finally learned the lesson that being busy doesn't equate to significant or value-adding activities. Filling time with tasks that don't have worth or meaning is something you can reverse with planning and self-reflection. Track the moments in your workday and non-workdays to see how you are truly spending your time. Consider how you can be more selective with your time and focus on what really matters in your life and career.

Stop the Busy Brag

Being busy is not something to celebrate, and we must reverse this dangerous cultural phenomenon by resisting the urge to brag about how busy we are. The busy brag is pervasive, but you can be a role model for others and share what gives you meaning and fulfillment instead of defaulting to telling others how busy you are. Start by actively listening, and when you hear a busy bragger, avoid the urge to chime in.

Some workplaces perpetuate the workaholic culture and praise the busy brag. This is not healthy or sustainable and often leads to a revolving door for talent that is neither cost-effective nor morale-boosting. In order to disrupt an antiquated workplace model, leaders must set an example and be willing to break or reinvent the HR mold.

Innovative companies like Netflix and Virgin Group are having great success offering flexible schedules and unlimited vacation time. It has helped them attract and retain top talent and avoid a workaholic culture while still demanding high productivity and results from their talent pool. Accountability lies with the individual employee.

Leaders must have candid conversations with employees to encourage them to take time off to rest, rejuvenate, and experience the health benefits that come with time away from work. Setting an example by not emailing, texting, or calling after regular business hours will help create and maintain a healthy work environment with lasting results for productivity and retention.

Busy Isn't Always Productive

Being busy just for the sake of face time or visibility in your workplace does not promote a healthy or wise culture for advancement and productivity in an organization. The concept of working smarter, not harder, is not new, and if organizations adopt these principles, it will foster productivity, efficiency, and overall satisfaction on the part of the worker.

Sprints, for example — focused and intense work sessions to accomplish a task or goal — are becoming mainstream beyond the high-tech organizations where this work style was born. Consider how you can hunker down and get work done during your unique sweet spot time of day. Then use the other time to recharge, tackle less intense tasks, and give your brain a chance to reboot. Your creativity, attention span, and productivity will soar. This also works outside of work.

Have Some Fun

Not a single person in my informal social experiment told me they were busy playing or having fun. Adults have lost the ability to play with reckless abandon like children do. This is one of the best ways to boost creativity, engage your brain, and release stress.

Consider how you can reintroduce play into your daily life. How can you play with no agenda and revel in what might be silly, effortless, and fun?

Savvy professionals will also incorporate playtime at work to encourage brain breaks, stimulate in-person communication amongst colleagues, and add a bit of levity to a stressful workday.

Being Still, Not Idle

As a high-energy person, I used to find it difficult to navigate downtime. Because I was not comfortable being inactive, I would fill the time with things to keep myself busy, and this exacerbated my stress.

While I am still working on being mindful and adding moments to my admittedly short meditations, I am becoming more comfortable being still. I am resisting the urge to find something to busy myself, and I am relishing the moments of calm, quiet, and stillness to reflect. I've come to understand that being still does not mean I'm lazy, and it has opened an opportunity to choose how I spend the unscheduled moments and give myself permission not to fill time with busy bunk.

Work Martyrs and Workaholics are Obsolete

As a Gen X professional, many of my career role models were driven and competitive baby boomers who worked themselves into debilitated health. My new intention is to focus on being a high achiever who can be results-driven without guilt and enjoy all the benefits of downtime.

Suffering is optional, and modern careerists have a choice. Busyness is not a badge of honor. Meaningless tasks that bring stress and drudgery do not make life more significant. Don't fritter away your time with unnecessary busy work.

Join me in the quest to abolish the busy brag and focus on a life and career with meaning, value, and joy. Don't forget to add playtime to your day and reach out to your accountability partners for support and encouragement.

PRO TIPS

- Remember that busy isn't always productive.

- Consider how you can be more selective with your time and focus on what really matters in your life and career.

- Learn to be still and relish moments of calm and quiet to reflect.

- Don't be a work martyr — give yourself permission to step away.

- Add playtime to your day for meaning and joy.

- Find accountability partners to help you stave off the busyness temptation.

CHAPTER **28**

TEAMWORK REBOOT

C hange is ubiquitous, and the world of work is evolving at a relentless speed. Hybrid work environments, labor shortages, and the fact that over half of the workforce is looking for new roles have made creating team culture a moving target. Given these factors, it's time to rethink how you lead a team and what you should consider when initiating a teamwork reboot.

Delegate

As a leader, it's important to cultivate and encourage talent on your team. Passing along a project is one way to do this. It creates an opportunity for someone else to develop as a leader, hone new skills, and take ownership of something that can showcase their strengths.

- Sharing key tasks demonstrates to team members that you have confidence in their abilities.

- Allowing direct reports to tackle next-level responsibilities that align with their interests and talents gives them hope for moving up in the future, as well as the assurance that you're invested in their career path.

- Providing one-on-one coaching and training will allow you to deepen your relationship with each person, allowing for a more cohesive team environment and strengthening the opportunity to delegate based on individual interests and skills.

Honor the 4 Cs of Communication

Teams thrive or fail based on how well they communicate. Sarah Goff-Dupont provides simple tactics that will enhance your virtual and in-person communication. [31]

- **Clear** – Avoid ambiguity. Anticipate any knowledge gaps in your audience and fill in the blanks for them. Avoid jargon. Use vocabulary that everyone will understand.

- **Concise** – Short, direct sentences are easier to follow than long, rambling thoughts. Avoid filler words that clutter the message. In writing, use bullet points and paragraph breaks to organize the text, but go easy on the exclamation marks. Your words should do the work, not your punctuation.

- **Correct** – People count on you to be truthful, so fact-check yourself. If you don't know the answer, say you'll find out instead of making something up. You'll be seen as a trustworthy source that others can rely on.

- **Compassionate** – Be courteous and kind when communicating. Your integrity and kindness will make you a person that others will want to listen to and engage with.

Please Stop Talking

Honing your communication skills takes self-awareness and practice, but it can also be a team sport. Be mindful of how your colleagues and direct reports communicate and how you can be of assistance, tapping your radical candor insight from an earlier chapter. When all team members have strong communication skills — the team shines together. One supportive team leader suggested that a direct report seek additional help to improve their communication skills, which is how I met Denver.

Denver is a client who came to me because he knew he had a proclivity for rambling. This communication flaw was holding him back from career advancement opportunities and came up regularly in his performance evaluations. When I was singing professionally, it was common practice to record a voice lesson or an opera rehearsal so I could play it back and learn about how to improve my technique, much like pro athletes study films to improve their game.

I started by recording Zoom team meetings led by Denver. He had never seen or heard himself ramble, and the audio/video recordings were quite humbling. I helped him adjust his body language to project a more assertive posture and unleash a more commanding tone, which also helped him ramp up his self-confidence.

I then asked him to write transcripts of his communication from the Zoom recordings so he could read what he said. The exercises were disarming and helped Denver see and hear what others were perceiving and incentivized him to adjust quickly. Denver is a stellar writer, so his communications immediately improved when he composed remarks in writing first and then edited them. He also identified a trusted accountability partner at work who could give him a subtle visual queue in real time when he slipped into old habits.

Over time, Denver learned to listen to himself and self-edit on the spot. He mastered the power of the pause and committed to scripting his remarks whenever possible to create new muscle memory for brevity and clarity. He delivered his remarks in a conversational way, so the scripting was undetectable. Denver is now helping others sharpen their communication skills and has been recognized as a strong verbal communicator.

Empathy Rules!

Empathy has been described as walking a mile in another's shoes, while sympathy is saying, "I'm sorry your feet hurt." Understanding someone else's perspective is an essential aspect of a teamwork reboot, and empathy is an important part of that connection.

Practice empathy by taking the time to ask colleagues how they are and really listen to the response. Don't make assumptions or judgments. Activate these empathetic behaviors regularly:

- Listen actively.
- Ask questions.

- Be approachable and available.
- Personalize your responses.
- Be observant and recognize what each team member needs and how they want to be recognized for great work.

Define the Problem Before Creating a Solution

Avoid creating a solution in search of a problem. Accurately defining a problem should be a team sport. Exploring a problem from different points of view almost always leads to a cleaner solution. Take the time to fully understand a challenge from different angles. Consider bringing in additional stakeholders to gain deeper clarity and entertain different points of view.

Clarify Priorities

The blurring of personal and professional boundaries has exacerbated burnout and employee disengagement. Use a sharp scalpel (metaphorically) to determine top priorities and what is truly urgent on your to-do list. By clarifying what is urgent, you will work smarter, not harder, and schedule tasks in a time-sensitive manner.

Everything can't be imperative at once, or it dilutes the concept of urgency. Help others beyond the team understand timelines and clarity of expectations, which will result in greater team morale, healthier colleagues, enhanced productivity, and better quality of work.

Design Your Team Culture Together

Given the rapid changes in the workplace over the last few years, the career landscape still seems abnormal in many ways. A team culture should not be dictated or mandated. It should be developed together, with buy-in from all team members.

Invest in your team by listening and learning about the culture they want to create and model for others. Your dream team will emerge when the team members are given the opportunity to help design it.

PRO TIPS

- Rethink how you lead or play on a team.

- Delegate more to allow others to take ownership and develop new skills.

- Be clear, concise, correct, and compassionate in your communication.

- Lead with empathy — ask colleagues how they are and really listen to the response.

- Define the problem before creating a solution.

- Design your team culture together.

CHAPTER 29

SINGLETASK TO A BETTER LIFE AND CAREER

Multitasking used to be a sought-after professional competency and was thought to be a valuable skill for busy professionals. Research tells us that singletasking is more effective and can result in higher productivity and time efficiency.

Envision the busy professional (maybe it's you?) working at their desk, reading this book while eating their lunch, checking their email, listening to a webinar, and texting their daughter about the change in her evening soccer practice. In the reality of overscheduled lives and careers, who has enough time to singletask?

We understand the danger of texting while driving, yet we knowingly overload our brains with multiple tasks every day.

This leads to a cluttered life and a growing list of unattainable and stressful demands on our day. Alas, there is hope for the myriad of multitaskers that long for a simpler and more productive life. Breathe deeply and read on.

Multitasking Myth

The human brain can only focus on one thing at a time. It is common for people to *task switch* — to move rapidly and ineffectively among tasks. Performance suffers when attention shifts back and forth in this way, as cited in Devora Zack's book, *Singletasking: Get More Things Done—One Thing at a Time.*[32]

Simplicity of Singletasking

Focusing on one thing until it's completed allows you to concentrate fully. It enables you to complete the task at hand faster and more accurately than if you were juggling multiple projects. An example of this type of scheduling would be to set aside specific blocks of time for email during your workday (this includes reading emails as well as composing or responding). Instead of spending precious time throughout the day stopping what you're working on to check email, the efficiency of these scheduled time blocks will free up time for you to do other things. It can also help to teach your audience (personal and professional) about your boundaries and set expectations for realistic response times.

Control Your Environment

I used to be like a Pavlovian dog with a visceral response to the audio ping of a new email, text, or meeting request on my Outlook calendar. Devora Zack explains how easy it is to control your environment and eliminate, or at least minimize, the visual and audio stimuli that cause you to lose focus. Adjust the settings on your computer and smartphone, so the sound is deactivated. Limiting screen time is not just for kids. Minimize your screen and device time to honor the environment you need to focus fully by adjusting the settings and setting boundaries.

Be More Mindful

Diane Sieg, a mindfulness practitioner, speaker, author, and founder of the Resilience Academy, shared: "Stress reduction and mindfulness don't just make us happier and healthier; they're a proven competitive edge that affects your bottom line." Mindfulness reduces the cost of employee turnover and sick leave, increases performance and productivity, and helps you feel energized more of the time, according to statistics by the iOpener Institute. "Mindfulness is a simple concept — the practice of being aware of your experiences in the present moment," according to Sieg, and a great strategy for the practice of mindfulness is singletasking.[33]

Singletask to Weight Loss

When was the last time you really tasted your food? How often have you eaten lunch at your desk or wolfed down something between meetings and didn't take the time to enjoy — or even taste — your food?

I love the concept of the slow food movement, where meals are hand-prepared from scratch for an artisanal culinary experience. Honor your body and singletask the next time you ingest food or drink. Experience eating with all five senses and make enjoying your food a single task. Chances are you will slow the eating process, become full faster, and eat less in the long run. Singletasking may just help you shed a few pounds without any extra work!

Reclaim Your Life

My friend, who has three teenage kids, has a house rule that all digital devices are put in a basket and shut off during family mealtimes. This digital detox allows the family to be fully present and experience the single task of eating together while enjoying each other's company. This not only means that they are making the most of precious family time, but it also models for her teens how to set boundaries and take control of their time.

Consider how you can begin to reclaim precious time by singletasking and staying more in the moment, whether at work or with loved ones. Singletasking empowers better active listening, more authentic experiences, and heightened focus so you can be fully in the present moment.

Less Is More

It's not about working harder — it's about working smarter. And being busy does not equate with being important or valuable.

Let go of the busyness of multitasking. Allow yourself to focus on fewer things and do them extraordinarily well instead of doing many things in a mediocre fashion.

I'm a singletasking work in progress, but even my initial baby steps have reduced my stress and helped me focus on what matters. Be kind to yourself and give yourself permission to slow down and tackle one thing at a time. You deserve it!

PRO TIPS

- Let go of multitasking and allow yourself to focus on doing fewer things extraordinarily well instead of doing many things in a mediocre fashion.

- The human brain can only focus on one thing at a time — honor the neuroscience and simplify to work smarter, not harder.

- Reclaim precious time by singletasking and staying more in the moment.

- Give yourself permission to slow down and tackle one task at a time.

FUTURE-PROOF YOUR CAREER

Sought-After Leaders Continue to Develop

CHAPTER 30

AN ENTREPRENEURIAL MINDSET

The world of work continues to change. Savvy leaders must hone their emotional intelligence to advance their own careers and recruit and retain top talent with a future-focused mindset. This section reveals what the future of work looks like and how you can create your distinct advantage.

In my work as an executive coach, I often help candidates prepare for pinnacle leadership role interviews. Sought-after leaders must continue to hone their emotional intelligence to honor the changing workplace dynamics and the professionals who work there.

While every leadership role requires nuanced experience and subject matter expertise relevant to the opportunity, I believe an entrepreneurial mindset is essential for all leaders. You need not be the founder of a start-up company or a business owner to think and act like an entrepreneur. Instead, you can tap and hone your intrapreneurial skills by developing new projects or products, fostering innovation, and setting a vision within a company.

Entrepreneurial Traits

Entrepreneurial traits can be learned and sharpened to help you pursue a fulfilling career, and they can also be very useful for teaching others in your sphere of influence. Even if you don't think of yourself as an entrepreneur or intrapreneur, the following qualities are also essential for excellent leaders. We can all learn a great deal from these entrepreneurial leadership traits.

Optimism – Radiates hopefulness and confidence about the future or the successful outcome of something. The pandemic forced us to live in a state of ambiguity. Optimism can be a guiding light during uncertain times and constant change. Optimism hones the art of the possible.

Self-Discipline – Empowers you to achieve. This multilayered competency includes:

- Commitment – Be true to your word.
- Taking care of yourself – Honor your mind, body, spirit, and well-being.
- Setting boundaries – Establish personal and professional limits that align with your values.
- Clearly defining goals – Specificity adds to the greater possibility of accomplishment.
- Honoring deadlines – Practice "good enough to go" by being brave, not perfect.

Open-Mindedness – Enables you to think critically and rationally and step out of your comfort zone to consider other ideas and perspectives.

Competitive Spirit – Focuses on your personal best as the healthiest form of competition. A competitive spirit can spark creativity, motivate you, increase productivity, and provide insight into how you navigate your strengths and blind spots.

Self-Motivation – Transforms your inner drive into action. This pushes you to keep going and be self-directed and proactive instead of relying on others to tell you what to do. It takes moxie and inner hutzpah to design your path forward.

Willingness to Fail – Learns from each mistake by being unafraid to fail forward — fast and often. Approach each day with a beginner's mind and learn to innovate and build resilience with each fabulous fail. Leaders who create an environment of psychological safety destigmatize failure and empower others to try new things.

Innovation – Implements new ideas that successfully lead to efficiency, effectiveness, and a competitive edge. Challenge your colleagues and organization to do things that will add value and improve the work, processes, or culture.

Tenacity – Taps your inner grit! Your firmness of mind and spirit and your unyielding courage in the face of challenge.

Flexibility – Adjusts to change quickly, willingly, and calmly so you can deal with unexpected problems and tasks effectively.

Ingenuity – Relies on your creative brainpower, which allows you to be clever, original, and inventive.

Willingness to Take Action – Puts your plan into action. In the spirit of design thinking, test-drive prototypes and iterate, as needed, even as early-stage prototypes. Action leads to growth and results; inaction leads to analysis paralysis.

Whether you are honing your leadership skills or interviewing with a potential leader for a new career opportunity you are considering, be mindful of the importance of an entrepreneurial spirit.

PRO TIPS

- An entrepreneurial mindset is essential for all leaders, whether you started the company or serve within it.

- Entrepreneurial traits can be learned and honed to help you pursue a fulfilling career and to groom others in your sphere of influence.

- Ignite your optimism to hone the art of the possible.

- Activate your competitive spirit — the healthiest form of competition focuses on your personal best.

- Fail forward, fast and often. Learn from each mistake and hone your resiliency.

- Be flexible and adjust to change quickly so you can deal with unexpected problems and tasks effectively.

- In the spirit of design thinking, put your plan into action, even as an early-stage prototype, to test-drive and iterate.

CHAPTER **31**

KICK IMPOSTER SYNDROME IN THE ASS

I mposter syndrome is an internal psychological experience in which an individual doubts their abilities, talents, or accomplishments and has a persistent internalized fear of being exposed as a fraud. The key word is internalized since it's a feeling you alone have about your value and worth. Studies indicate that 83 percent of working adults experience imposter syndrome, and it is particularly common in high-achieving women.

It boils down to lacking consistent self-confidence. Combating this requires overcoming doubt, insecurity, and fear in order to improve your thinking and change behaviors to release the emotions that hold you back.

Self-confidence is a precious asset, and I hear from many who don't feel confident at work. It's essential to break down the foundation of self-confidence to understand how it works. There are specific action steps you must put into practice to own this often-elusive competency. Like any skill, it takes intentionality and practice, and this chapter will show you how.

Self-confident professionals feel assured their work is of high quality. They also feel comfortable participating in meetings and discussions. Confident people don't overthink or second-guess themselves, and they are willing to explore new things and take on new challenges.

What's holding you back from feeling confident? Low self-esteem is often the culprit. Confidence and self-esteem go hand in hand. Self-esteem is your overall opinion of yourself, while confidence is trusting your own abilities. Building up your confidence at work can also help to increase your self-esteem, and there are several steps you can take to work toward that goal.

Own Your Situation

You must recognize your personal responsibility for how you feel about yourself. Start by being kind to yourself and stop beating yourself up with self-blaming and self-shaming. This negative pattern of behaviors can lead to long-term conditioning that is hard to reprogram. It's time to get out of these negative thought patterns and focus on a growth mindset.

A growth mindset is action-oriented and focuses on these areas:

- A desire to keep learning
- Belief in yourself
- Ability to take calculated risks
- Bias toward action

- Courage to accept new challenges and opportunities
- A sense of self-discipline
- A focus on what's positive

When you practice a growth mindset, you give yourself permission to learn new things and take a chance on something new based on your *potential* to learn. You give yourself permission to mitigate the fear of what you don't currently know and own that you can learn something new. The difference between an imposter syndrome mindset and a growth mindset is slight but significant.

Imposter Syndrome Mindset: "I don't know what I'm doing. It's only a matter of time until everyone finds out."

Growth Mindset: "I don't know what I'm doing *yet*. It's only a matter of time until I figure it out.

Both of these statements acknowledge that there are often things we don't know. The difference is that a growth mindset believes knowledge is possible. In fact, the highest form of self-confidence is believing in your ability to learn.

Acknowledge Your Self Worth

You have great value. You have career experience, education, and specialized training, and you work hard! Remind yourself about what you do well. Journal your accomplishments and ask those in your circle of trust to share what they believe you do well so you can trust that others see your value as well. Commit to strengthening your confidence muscles and owning your strengths and accomplishments on a regular basis. Think of professional athletes who condition, train, and practice their sport outside of competition seasons to stay strong, focused, and prepared. It takes a commitment to acknowledge and feed your self-confidence so it can thrive. Look yourself in the mirror and begin your day with the affirmation, "I can do this!" and celebrate how awesome you are.

It's essential to be realistic and embrace your imperfections, knowing that as a human being, you are not, nor will you ever be, perfect. Welcome to humanity. Since perfection is impossible (think brave, not perfect), you must be honest about your imperfections, mistakes, and failures to drive your learning and growth.

Failure Deconstruction

When you fail or make a mistake, consider what you learned. Pay attention and get specific with how you respond and recover. Make a choice to adopt a growth mindset. Determine when to invest in training and development and learn to recognize when the thing that you failed at was not a good investment of your strengths and energy from the start.

Failure does not mean you are broken. Perfection doesn't exist. Investing in activities and a career that honors your strengths is smart and essential. If you are in a role where you are constantly asked to improve or fix something, chances are you are in the wrong role. Don't invest time ramping up your weaknesses. This is a self-confidence killer. Focus on what you do well, and seek opportunities to do more of it, and take it to a higher level to maximize the strengths and talents you have.

Achieving Goals to Gain Self-Confidence

If you recognize that you lack self-confidence, it's time to reverse your thought process. Setting and achieving goals can help you prove to yourself that you have value. You must commit to setting and achieving the goals for this to work. Take an incremental approach to train your way to lasting self-confidence. Work your way up from a small goal to what Jim Collins refers to in his book, *Built to Last*, as a Big Hairy Audacious Goal (BHAG), as follows:[34]

Small Win: Create a defined, simple, reachable goal that will help you move forward in a short period of time — a few hours or a day. Example: Reach out to a LinkedIn contact to set up an informational interview about a role in a company you have been considering where your contact now works.

SMART Goal: Specific, Measurable, Aligned, Reachable, and Time-Bound. This may take a few weeks or maybe a month. Example: Submit a proposal to speak at a national conference in six months. You are a subject matter expert in your industry and meet the call for proposals criteria. The timeframe gives you ample time to prepare, and serving as a speaker will up your visibility in your organization (and beyond). It also may put you in the running for promotion.

BHAG - Big Hairy Audacious Goal: Dream BIG and give yourself permission to take a risk on something you care about, even if it scares you. Tap your

imagination and reflect on what will help you feel purpose, meaning, and fulfillment in your life and career.
This will likely take longer and require planning and
execution — several months or even a year. Perhaps
you aspire to give a TEDx Talk, run a marathon, or
write a book. Dreaming big will launch your creativity
and empower your self-confidence.

Comfort Zones

You have heard about getting out of your comfort zone to try
something new and stretch yourself. When you are inside your
comfort zone, you are experiencing what you already *do*. When
you are outside your comfort zone, you try experiencing what you
want, even if you are fearful or doubt your success. By stretching
beyond what you are accustomed to doing, you build new confidence muscles. The muscle memory develops, and what used
to cause fear or self-doubt is now securely in your comfort zone
and will enhance your self-confidence.

Honor a growth mindset — the more you try new things, the
more you will grow your self-confidence.

Sustaining Your Self-Confidence

Who do you spend time with? Who feeds you energy? Who
stresses you out? Consider who you surround yourself with and
how they make you feel. How you feel is a resource you must
protect, and you have control over who you choose to spend your
time with.

If there is a difficult person at work, limit the interaction you have with that person so they don't drain your energy and send you into a spiral of self-doubt. Seek out positive people who appreciate your work and feed your energy with authenticity. This technique also applies to your personal life. Connect with people who lift your spirits, make you laugh, and make you feel good about yourself.

To feed your positivity and sustain your self-confidence, get clear about what you want to achieve and visualize it. Create a vision board or write in a journal and reflect on what crossing the finish line of your goal looks and feels like. And be specific. The more you can visualize your achievement, the more you can work to make it happen. Your achievements are hard evidence that you are valuable and an essential step to kicking imposter syndrome in the ass.

Real-Time Self-Confidence Boosters

If you need a quick self-confidence boost, here are some easy-to-implement action steps to help you reverse a negative thought process and focus on owning your value.

- Check in with a mentor, coach, friend, or accountability partner for a mental reset from negative to positive.
- Start your day with meaningful work — ignite your positivity. Track the meaningful work and see how it impacts your self-confidence.
- Celebrate a win or achievement with a tangible reward like a special coffee drink, a new book you have wanted to read, or dinner out with friends or a loved one.

The Obnoxious Roommate in Your Head

Stop renewing the lease for the obnoxious roommate of self-doubt that lives in your head and eats away at your self-confidence. Your superego is the obnoxious roommate spewing self-doubt, and this behavior has been deeply ingrained from an early age.

The Freudian theory of the *superego* comes from the internalized ideas that we have acquired from our parents, family, and society. This voice in your head started at an early age, and it can be difficult to ignore now. This voice does not come from reason, logic, or intelligence, and you can separate yourself from it. Old habitual thinking needs to be updated and reprogrammed to make room for self-confidence.

Perhaps you were taught from an early age to be humble and not boast about your accomplishments. This will directly impact how you articulate your value in the career world. You are most likely selling yourself short because your *superego* is beckoning you to showcase humility.

Maybe you were taught that it was inappropriate to talk about money and how much people earn. You can see the correlation to negotiating on your own behalf when discussing the salary for a new role. There is societal inequity in salaries due to a lack of transparency in the world of work — much of which may be rooted in the *superego*. As you can see, the impact can be huge.

You must reprogram your *superego* to remove self-doubt, kick out the obnoxious roommate in your brain, and give yourself space to own your self-confidence. Focus on thoughts and emotions that come from reasoning, logic, and facts. Be cognizant that stress activates and feeds outdated *superego* narratives.

Change your behaviors by gaining new experiences, setting new patterns, and focusing on growth zone exercises to let your confidence re-emerge.

PRO TIPS

- Practice a growth mindset to give yourself permission to learn new things and take a chance on something new based on your *potential*.

- The highest form of self-confidence is believing in your ability to learn.

- Commit to strengthening your confidence muscles and owning your strengths and accomplishments on a regular basis.

- Look yourself in the mirror and begin your day with the affirmation, "I can do this!" Celebrate how awesome you are.

- Embrace your imperfections, knowing that as a human being, you are not, nor will you ever be, perfect.

- Focus on what you do well and seek opportunities to do more of it. Then take it to a higher level to maximize your strengths and talents.

CHAPTER 32

CAN YOU HEAR ME NOW?

In the last ten years, the human attention span has decreased from 12 seconds to 8 seconds. Goldfish have a 9-second attention span. Ponder that. Goldfish can pay attention longer than some humans. And the situation has been exacerbated by the overstimulation of too many meetings and not enough processing and creative thinking time. Active listening is an important component of attention and is an essential emotional intelligence competency that will distinguish you in the career world. The good news is that it is a learned skill we all can hone.

Can You Hear Me Now?

We've all been in situations when the person we are speaking to is zoning out and not fully grasping what we are saying. It's frustrating and is a problem that has been accelerated by multitasking, the constant tether to our smart devices, meetings while driving, and camera-off Zoom calls without eye contact. But it also happens in face-to-face scenarios, so we can't blame it entirely on remote work or digital communication.

I've worked in organizations where most participants in a meeting were on their phones or laptops while supposedly listening to remarks during the session. The blatant lack of listening was rude and set the tone for the organizational culture.

Listening is a skill and a clear demonstration of how much you care. It's not a passive action. To stay engaged and ensure clear communication, it's essential to practice active listening, which Kat Boogaard defines as follows:[35]

> Active listening means listening to someone else with the intent of hearing them, understanding their message, and retaining what they say. Think of active listening as the most engaged and committed form of listening to another person. Beyond just hearing them, you're giving them your full attention while signaling to the speaker that their message is being received and comprehended. It also helps you, as the listener, to engage with and understand the message more effectively.

The Gift of Your Undivided Attention

You may only need your ears to hear, but you need your whole brain to listen. Giving someone your undivided attention is a true gift. The unconditional focus on what they are saying takes time, concentration, and respect. You must remove distractions and listen to understand.

Empathy is also part of active listening — putting yourself in the speaker's shoes and trying to understand their point of view. You need not agree, but you should honor the speaker's opportunity to share a point.

Introverts and Extraverts

As an extravert, I am energized by people. I often think out loud and, on occasion, must revise what I say since my mouth can engage faster than my brain. My executive coach encourages me to "listen to listen" and not to respond.

Practicing this has been a game changer for my active listening and liberated my extraverted personality to take a beat, so I listen more and talk less.

My introverted colleagues, friends, and family members take time to process what they hear before they speak. But there is a cultural bias toward extraverts since they tend to be the first to speak up or ask a question. Extraverts can also be the first to interrupt, which is the exact opposite of active listening.

I'm committed to being more proactive about this unfair bias and honoring silence as I continue to hone my active listening skills. We can celebrate both personality types as active listeners and be cognizant of how we offer visual cues of acknowledgment — think head nods, smiling, or eye contact — when someone else is speaking. Active listening requires self-awareness of our own behavior in how we engage with the person speaking.

True Understanding

Active listening takes us to a deeper level of understanding and can offer the listener a chance to ask for clarification. Try rephrasing what the other person said to reassure the speaker that you are listening and provide an opportunity for clarification.

For example: "What I heard you say is X. Is that accurate?" Meaning can often be lost in delivery or interpretation, so it's better to be sure to align in real-time rather than risk letting a missed message gather dust.

It's not what you say; it's what they hear.

A Tactical Approach to Listening

Prepare to listen – Reboot your attention and focus on the other person with fresh ears and an open mind. This is also important in a group setting or if you are an audience member listening to a speaker.

Observe the verbal and nonverbal cues – You must listen with both your eyes and your ears since 55 percent of communication is nonverbal. Remember that, as the listener, your nonverbal cues are equally important. How are you showing your undivided attention with your body language? Honor the speaker with your eye contact and open (uncrossed) arms to signal that you are focused on what they are saying. Nod your head occasionally to show you are engaged.

Engage in two-way communication – Providing feedback, asking questions, rephrasing key points, and taking notes not only help you retain what you heard but also show the speaker that you are engaged.

Why Active Listening Matters

There are many benefits to active listening. They include:

Improved Relationships – We can all relate to a time when someone we care about was not fully focused on our important message. The term *selective listening* makes me bristle. Consider how you feel when someone gives you the gift of their full and undivided attention. It boosts your self-confidence, makes you feel valued and recognized, and enhances trust in a relationship.

Better Understanding – Let's not ignore the obvious — active listening allows for deeper understanding and comprehension. There is an advertising paradigm that states people need to hear something at least seven times before they grasp the concept. Perhaps we can reduce that number if we engage in more active listening.

Bias Reduction – The workplace spotlight is currently focused on diversity, equity, and inclusion and the awareness and mitigation of bias — both conscious and unconscious. Active listening helps us step outside of our own point of view and see things from the speaker's perspective. It reduces assumptions and allows for a deeper understanding when we truly "listen to listen."

Become an Active Listener

As you work toward becoming a more active listener, there are some steps you can take to help set the stage for success:

- **Mitigate distractions.** Put down your smartphone and turn off the message prompts and audible pings on your devices that can pull your focus away.
- **Check your emotions of the day at the door.** Begin the conversation with a clean slate so you can listen with an open mind. Turn off the monkey chatter in your brain.
- **Have clarity about your actual attention span.** While a five-minute meeting isn't realistic, if you can only hold focus for 30 minutes, be clear with friends and colleagues that a shorter engagement will lead to a more meaningful interaction with you.
- **Don't jump to solutions.** Our job as listeners is not always to provide a solution — sometimes, people just want to be heard. Let the speaker guide the conversation and ask for input or solutions, so you can focus on listening.
- **Engage your body language as you listen.** Eye contact, positive facial expressions, and an alert posture all indicate that you are listening fully to the speaker.
- **Don't interrupt.** I'll say it again — "listen to listen" and not to respond. There will be a time for you to engage in the conversation but wait and take the cue from the speaker.

When was the last time you felt like someone gave you the gift of their true and undivided attention? This gift is free and is yours to develop and hone, so active listening can be a hallmark of your emotional intelligence and leadership behavior.

PRO TIPS

- Listen to listen and not to respond.

- Active listening is the most engaged and committed form of listening to another person. By giving your full attention, you are signaling that their message is being received and comprehended.

- Activate your empathy as part of active listening. Put yourself in the speaker's shoes and try to understand their point of view.

- It's not what you say; it's what they hear.

- Mitigate distractions — to enhance your active listening, check your emotions at the door, engage your body language as you listen, and don't interrupt.

- This gift of your undivided attention is free and yours to develop and hone as a hallmark of your emotional intelligence and leadership behavior.

CHAPTER 33

EARNING RESPECT VS. BEING LIKED

I t is human nature to want to be liked at work, but I urge you to go the extra mile to earn the respect of your colleagues and your boss. There is a difference between being liked and respected in a leadership role. If you earn the respect of your team, they will be more accountable and productive, and they will be more likely to go the extra mile for you.

In the era of Instagram and ubiquitous social media, you can "like" something with the click of a mouse to show your attraction or acknowledgment of a person, object, or sentiment in a post. It has become a popularity contest of sorts to attract numerous likes and expand your social media presence and network of friends.

Many people get sucked into the popularity contest mindset in the workplace as well and strive to be liked by their colleagues. It's natural to say that you want to be liked and respected, but you must work hard to earn the trust and respect of others. It's not gratuitous, and it takes time.

Nice is Not Enough – Being courteous and professional in the workplace is expected. But being nice must also have guard rails. Nobody ever earned kudos on a performance evaluation for being nice. And if you are passive and overly agreeable, it may hinder your chances of getting promoted or working on prime assignments. Being overly nice is probably not in your job description, so don't allow yourself to be exploited by succumbing to this self-sabotaging behavior.

Professional Respect – This is a positive feeling of esteem or deference for a person and their actions. You have to assert yourself to be seen and heard so you can be recognized for the great work you are accomplishing. If you are cultivating a professional persona where you are indispensable at work and make others aware of your talents, you can become the go-to expert and distinguish yourself amongst your peers. This is a two-way street — to be respected, you need to treat everyone with dignity and respect. Period.

Friends or Enemies? Charlotte Beers, former chairman and CEO of Ogilvy & Mather Worldwide, says that relationships often matter more than work. Perhaps that doesn't seem fair, but it's a reality. The quality of your work may be trumped by the relationships you build or break. Beers states:[36]

> You must recognize that there will be a moment in time when you will not be able to be represented by the quality of your work but

rather by the relationships you have. Make as few enemies as possible; it's really just good form. Men can compete ferociously with each other and then turn around and lend a hand to their opponent. Here's the bottom line: The person who is very good at relationships is the one who gets to be in charge.

It's a small world, and your boss today may be your customer in a year. Every person counts in our connected world of work, and respect is a key element in maintaining professional relationships.

Teach People How to Treat You

Be clear about how you want people to treat you. You have so much more control over this than you are allowing yourself to use. Negotiate your relationships to get what you want. Give yourself permission to train the people around you (at work and at home), so they treat you with respect and dignity. You must take responsibility for shaping other people's behavior and teach them how you wish to be treated.

If you accept when people are aggressive, bossy, or controlling and they get their way, you have rewarded them for unacceptable behavior. You need to be assertive and ready to negotiate what you need and want in the workplace from a position of strength and power — not from fear or self-doubt. You must be uncompromising in your resolve to be treated with dignity and respect. Being nice is not enough to command the respect of others.

Action Steps for Earning Respect

Renowned national championship-winning high school wrestling coach John Klessinger wrote *A Coach's Manual,* which illustrates how a sports coach must earn the respect of their team because being liked is simply not enough. These rules of engagement to earn the respect of a team are as applicable in the career world as they are on the playing field. Klessinger recommends the following:[37]

1. Set the example with your enthusiasm, commitment, and dedication.
2. Mean what you say and say what you mean. If you say you are going to do it, do it. Your team will quickly see if you are a person of your word or just giving them "lip service."
3. Hold people accountable for your mission, standards, and expectations.
4. Show your human side — admit fault, own your mistakes, and have moments where you are vulnerable. Be willing to apologize and also show appreciation.
5. Treat everyone the same regarding team expectations. This means everyone follows the same standards. If your standards are to be on time, work hard, and have a positive attitude, then hold everyone accountable to those standards.
6. Be consistent in your messaging.
7. Develop trust and rapport.
8. Listen to your players and open lines of communication.

Self-Confidence is Empowering

As you navigate your career journey, consider how you can intentionally and authentically earn the respect of your colleagues. The goal is to be more assertive and self-assured but not aggressive. Your new commitment to earning respect will be palpable to others and perhaps cause a positive ripple effect in your organization. Don't ever compromise or sell out on this most precious commodity because you deserve to be respected.

A bonus to being respected at work is that people will enjoy being around you, and that's a good thing. You will continue to foster professional relationships at work, which only benefits your career in the long run.

PRO TIPS

- Give yourself permission to train the people around you (at work and at home) to treat you with respect and dignity.

- Consider how you can intentionally and authentically earn the respect of your colleagues.

- The goal is to be more assertive and self-assured but not aggressive.

- The quality of your work may be trumped by the relationships you build or break.

CHAPTER 34

THE TRUTH ABOUT
TALENT RETENTION

Values are the greatest predictor of career satisfaction, and the post-pandemic journey has caused a shift in values for many employees. Many companies are scrambling to retain top talent, and aside from the obvious financial and integrity cost of the burn and churn of employee turnover, company culture will continue to hang by a thread if leaders do not offer employees growth opportunities and create a place where people really want to work.

It's time to take employee retention seriously — to honor the great talent you have and attract the new talent you need. Whether you are a leader trying to keep your talented people in the company or one of the talented people looking to go elsewhere, there are lessons to be learned in this chapter.

Stay Interviews

If you are waiting for the annual performance review to under-stand your employees, you are missing the retention boat. I highly recommend a *stay interview*. This is a frequent conversation be-tween leader and employee and is a great opportunity for the leader to be an active listener and learn from the direct report about their ideas for progress, goals, solutions, and challenges. In turn, the leader will also have an opportunity to receive construc-tive feedback from the employee — a concept that's not always utilized in the more traditional one-way performance review.

Creating a safe environment of respect, candor, and authen-ticity is essential. Both the leader and the employee can com-fortably share constructive feedback. Here are some questions to get the conversation started:

- When you get ready for work each day, what things do you look forward to?
- What parts of your job are the most enjoyable? Are any parts fun?
- What parts are most challenging? What are your road-blocks or frustrations?
- What are you learning here? What do you want to learn?
- How do you like working with other members of our team?
- And what about me? What can I do more of? What should I stop doing? What should I start doing that I'm not do-ing now?
- What can I do to help you stay longer?
- Are there specific things you can think of that might cause you to leave?

Scott's Stay Interview Epiphany

A longtime client of mine, Scott discovered firsthand the power of a stay interview. Scott has grown his career from mid-level management to a senior executive role in healthcare. He leads a team of professionals who were weary from the overwhelm and exhaustion that was exacerbated by the pandemic. Scott introduced the stay interview as an informal check-in with his direct reports that complemented the annual performance evaluation — a vendor product that felt impersonal and boilerplate in his company. Each direct report is a manager who leads a team of their own.

His team was wary at first since these unofficial conversations required vulnerability and authenticity. Scott worked intentionally with his team to create psychological safety, and over time, the team developed a level of trust and a safe space that was noticed by other leaders and teams. The casual conversation prompts in the stay interview gave Scott's team of managers the opportunity to speak truth to power on a regular basis and share how they were feeling and what obstacles were in their way. Most importantly, it gave the managers a chance to share candid feedback about Scott and how he could empower them to do their best work.

During an unprecedented period of burnout and exhaustion, the stay interview conversations brought comfort to team members and to Scott as well. The process inspired radical candor and team-inspired solutions, and it morphed into weekly team huddles to discuss issues and to brainstorm. One manager shared that she finally felt seen and heard, and she asked Scott to encourage the chief human resources officer to make the stay interview available for all employees.

A stay interview is now an option for all in Scott's organization. Not every leader has embraced it, but those using stay interviews are retaining more employees, and it has moved the needle on employee engagement.

Provide Career Growth Opportunities

Most of the talented individuals who leave organizations do so because there is no opportunity for career growth or reinvention. Careers with meaning and purpose are high on the values list for many, and organizations that let the dust settle on stagnant job descriptions and outdated roles will most certainly lose out.

In addition to actual succession plans for leadership roles, companies should look at all rungs of the organizational chart. Are you tending to the frozen middle and the wealth of talent waiting for an opportunity to try something new, gain leadership experience, and develop professionally?

Innovative organizations create Emerging Leaders Boards, tapping young, entry-level talent so they can better understand the next generation of leaders and actively groom them for what's next. There is an additional benefit that comes from the reverse generational learning that takes place when bringing Gen Y (millennials) and Gen Z together with Gen X and baby boomers.

Create real opportunities for advancement, so top talent can grow from within instead of growing out of your organization.

Lighten the Load of Your Best People

I learned a strategic practice from the professional sports realm called load management. Winning sports coaches practice load management — a strategy to save the top talent for critical times.

They rest their stars during less important games to keep them fresh for playoffs or must-win games. This translates to the work world and is a savvy technique to retain your star performers.

Think about which of your employees are working the longest hours, coming in at weird times, answering your emails at midnight, etc. It's unlikely that your low performers are working anywhere near as hard as your best employees. Part of the fault lies with the leaders, who tend to always turn to the top employees when they need something done. You are not calling folks with bad attitudes; over and over, you tap your stars for help.

Perpetual overwork is debilitating. Honor your rock stars and give them a break. If you don't, they may look elsewhere for a more manageable work/life fit.

Culture Fit

People stay with an organization because of company culture alignment and strong leaders. For the values of an organization to have true meaning, they must be demonstrated by actions and not simply verbiage on the website.

Psychological safety is a must-have work culture competency so employees can do their work knowing they won't be punished or humiliated for speaking up with ideas, questions, concerns, or mistakes.

Organizations with desirable cultures tend to have things in common — they have clear goals, measurable performance indicators, and good communication, and they foster an environment of collaboration. They also have created a positive and inclusive workplace where all the employees are valued, supported, and nurtured, regardless of gender, sexual orientation, or race. All employees should have equal opportunities to progress and equal access to the rewards and perks available.

There's a question that's become my mantra: *Is this a place where you can do your best work?* It's imperative for leaders to take company culture seriously and incorporate the ideas of the people who are impacted the most — those who work in the organization. There is currently a talent war that is providing opportunities for professionals to move around — a lot. Changing roles frequently is no longer a red flag. Hungry hiring managers seek this knowledge transfer and entice top talent to consider other opportunities. Having the right culture can provide a significant advantage.

Talent retention is about creating a place where people want to work for the foreseeable future. Potential employees expect growth and professional development opportunities, workplace well-being, flexibility, and a commitment to diversity, equity, and inclusion. These have become deal breakers. Committing to these work culture elements is essential, and savvy leaders are putting them into practice to ensure they can attract and keep top talent.

PRO TIPS

- Utilize the stay interview technique to engage in radically candid conversations about the current state of individuals and what they need to be successful.

- Create real opportunities for advancement so top talent can grow from within instead of growing out of your organization.

- Encourage generational diversity to promote cross-learning that spans from entry-level to the executive team.

- Create an Emerging Leaders Board and tap young, entry-level talent to better understand the next generation of leaders and feed the leadership pipeline.

- Lighten the load of your best people and groom other star players, so you can honor the bench and not burn out your top talent.

CHAPTER **35**

HOW THE FUTURE *WORKS*

The pandemic turned the traditional nine-to-five workday on its head — out of necessity. The real-time global case study in remote/hybrid work has irrevocably changed how people want to work moving forward. With the worker's market driving change, savvy organizations are rethinking the way we work long-term in the new digital-first workplace.

This chapter title comes directly from a must-read book by Sheela Subramanian, Helen Kupp, and Brian Elliott, coauthors of *How the Future Works: Leading Flexible Teams to Do the Best Work of Their Lives.*[38] Sheela Subramanian and Helen Kupp, cofounders and executive leaders at Future Forum, joined me on my *Your Working Life* podcast to discuss how to unlock the power of flexible work to benefit the worker and the organization.

Flexibility Drives Satisfaction

Future Forum equips leaders to drive transformation at work, and their research cites flexibility as the most important driver of job satisfaction after compensation. Flexibility is not only about where you work but when you work. Scheduling flexibility is more important than location flexibility for many. According to Future Forum, office-knowledge workers, who have little or no ability to set their own work hours, are far more likely to look for a new job in the coming year compared to those with schedule flexibility.

The Great Disconnect

The root cause of the mass exodus of workers seeking new opportunities is that in many organizations, the executives and the employees are still not on the same page when it comes to flexible work. The disconnect is real.

Executives have always had more flexibility in their work and may not be cognizant of what is happening in the employee trenches.

Subramanian and Kupp share data points from a Future Forum study that shows the divide between leadership and employees:[39]

- Executives have a 62 percent higher rate of satisfaction than employees.
- Non-executive employees report twice as much work-related stress and anxiety.
- Approximately 68 percent of executives surveyed wanted to work in the office all or most of the time — three times the number of nonexecutives who said the same.

People from all levels of the organization must be involved in designing flexible work plans since there is no one-size-fits-all approach in the new world of work.

Bust the Flexible-Work Myths

The negative myths about flexible work are not backed up by data. Some express concern that flexible work will negatively impact productivity. Research shows the opposite — flexible work increases productivity. And many fear that work flexibility will inhibit growth, but this is not the case. It can actually lead to better creativity and innovation.

Some leaders also worry that flexible work will erode company culture and employee connectivity, but research indicates that flexibility is a critical tool in improving a sense of connection and belonging.

Diversity, Equity, Inclusion, and Belonging

We know that diverse teams outperform nondiverse teams by growing faster and being more innovative. Offering flexible work options encourages a greater diversity of applicants, which welcomes a wider talent pool for organizations seeking to fill critical roles, retain top talent, and build a leadership bench for succession planning. Subramanian and Kupp shared on my podcast that Dropbox saw a 16 percent increase in diverse candidates and three times the number of total applicants with flexible work offerings. And Slack hired one-third more remote-based historically discriminated employees than office-based.

Break Away from Perpetual Meetings

Nobody enjoys endless meetings that suck the oxygen out of a day and eliminate white space on the calendar to reflect, think creatively, and do the work. The coauthors of *How the Future Works* suggest the Four-D model, where meetings are only held when team members need to Discuss, Debate, Decide, and Develop.

Savvy companies like Google have "no meeting weeks." During Slack's "Maker Weeks," the company allows people to turn off notifications and relish meeting-free time to do focused work.

Instead of scheduling a traditional meeting, consider "core collaboration hours," where team members are available for synchronous collaboration. This unlocks more productivity than having set working hours when employees feel they need to be on all the time. These core hours can change based on the needs of the team.

Be Bold and Test-Drive

With flexible work and digital tools emerging as norms in many industries, leaders need to redefine the role of managers and reskill them for success. Investing in coaching, structured feedback, and recognition is a great start.

While flexible schedules may seem unrealistic or a mountain too high to climb in your organization, take a deep breath and consider a pilot program as an experiment. Tap an entrepreneurial spirit and design a prototype with input from all levels of the organization. Give it a test period to see what works and what doesn't, and then iterate to make it better.

It's clear that flexibility supports workplace health and well-being. The return on investment is better productivity and outcomes, as well as employee retention. The talent wars continue, and companies must be willing to rethink how people work to attract and retain a loyal workforce. If this sounds appealing but daunting, check out the "How the Future Works Toolkit" from Future Forum to create a framework for flexible work principles you can customize in your organization.

Building a culture of transparency and a willingness to try new things to empower employees to succeed will add to the engagement and retention of top talent. Flexibility as a core work value is not going away, and it will determine where people choose to work. Honoring flexibility is a smart way to future-proof your organization.

PRO TIPS

- To power transformation at work, flexibility is essential — it's the most important driver of job satisfaction after compensation.

- Build a culture of transparency and a willingness to try new things to increase engagement, empower employees to succeed, and retain top talent.

- Data shows that flexibility supports workplace health and well-being. The return on investment is better productivity and outcomes, as well as employee retention.

- Start incorporating flexible options as a prototype and allow for iteration to find the best solutions for the talent and the organization.

CONCLUSION

The world of work has irrevocably changed, and you have an opportunity to consciously design what you want your life and career to look like moving forward.

While the pandemic forced us to handle ambiguity out of necessity, it also provided an opportunity for us to reconsider what we value. The VUCA workplace (volatile, uncertain, complex, and ambiguous) is daunting and not an environment that attracts and retains top talent.

I choose to reframe VUCA and focus on the high-velocity workplace where you can make a positive change as an impact player. High-velocity professionals deliver results and continuously hone their emotional intelligence to be agile and resilient in the ever-changing world of work. The future is yours to design. How you establish boundaries, priorities, and the integration of life and work will influence the current and next generation of career professionals as well as your career satisfaction. Consider your future the art of the possible.

Behaviors and practices at work will continue to evolve, and you have an opportunity to be a positive change agent. You can impact the creation of healthy and sustainable work cultures where top talent is recognized and has an opportunity for growth, and work addiction is not celebrated. You can be integrally involved in succession planning (you may be the succession plan!) and setting the strategy for what happens next.

A Future-Proof Professional

While there is no guarantee you can completely future-proof your career against unknown changes in the economy, global health, and the political landscape, I hope this book has taught you how to continuously hone your emotional intelligence and agility, so you can adopt a growth mindset. Change is unavoidable, and you must be nimble and ready to pivot quickly to adapt and reset. Trust what you have learned in this book, and bravely put it into practice.

As a savvy professional, you will show up, speak up, brave up, and actively listen, offering others your undivided attention. Giving and receiving developmental feedback is now your superpower. A commitment to helping others grow becomes the norm.

Creating teams and workplaces with psychological safety, inclusivity, and a fail-forward mindset that inspires creative risk-taking is in your wheelhouse now. You are poised to be brave, not perfect, and allow individuals to bring their authentic selves to work, which impacts retention and career satisfaction.

You are ready to design your career trajectory with smart growth and seek or serve as a sponsor to pay it forward to someone with high potential. You understand the power of executive presence. You also recognize that sometimes less can be more — the outcome is often better when you focus on doing fewer things extraordinarily rather than doing everything in a mediocre fashion.

This book has taught you to diffuse conflict, embrace a coaching mindset with colleagues, and focus on resilience and recovery. You now lead with curiosity and an entrepreneurial mindset to prototype, test, and iterate in the spirit of design thinking.

Make It Better Now

Finally, my sincere hope is that this book has taught you that you deserve to have a livelihood that honors your life and career simultaneously. I have learned that I can prioritize time for my personal life without feeling guilty or succumbing to my former work addiction — and *still* be a high achiever. I hope my experience has helped you.

You have the awareness to prioritize white space on your calendar to allow for creative thought, reflection, and dreaming big. You won't wait for things to get better because you can make small, incremental changes now that will lead to powerful results and create an environment where you can do your best work and live your best life.

You now have a distinct *Career Advantage* and the knowledge, Pro Tips, and action steps to empower you to navigate a rewarding work and life journey. The opportunity to design your destiny is yours, so make sure it doesn't happen by default. Enjoy your career AND love your life!

ABOUT CAROLINE

Caroline Dowd-Higgins is passionate about helping individuals and organizations successfully adapt to today's complex, uncertain, and high-velocity work environments. Her coaching, writing, and speaking endeavors help leaders develop more collaborative, creative, entrepreneurial, and change-agile capabilities. She specializes in working with mid-career leaders, first-time C-suite leaders, and pinnacle role executives.

Caroline is a member of the International Coaching Federation and is certified as a LeaderShape Transpersonal Leadership Coach, a Marshall Goldsmith Stakeholder Centered Coach, and a Gallup-Certified Strengths Coach. Additional training includes the following frameworks: design thinking, shared equity leadership, mitigating bias, and creating inclusive cultures.

Caroline is passionate about unlocking the art of the possible, and her engaging and inspiring style helps people and organizations navigate change, overcome challenges, and elevate strengths so they can thrive. She has held executive leadership roles in organizations, so she knows firsthand the difficulties and opportunities found in a competitive career marketplace. Her client list includes organizations such as Eli Lilly, Salesforce,

Brocade, Meta, Cook Medical, BAIRD, Endress+Hauser, Deaconess Health, Sanofi, Rolls Royce, Nielsen, and Vision Three. She provides tools and resources to help develop healthy and sustainable work cultures with a focus on talent development, retention, and growth.

As a testimony to the power of transferable skills, prior to working as a leader in the corporate, higher education, and non-profit sectors and establishing her coaching, speaking, and consulting practice, Caroline worked as a professional opera singer in Europe and the United States. She knows the power of career reinvention and is adept at helping individuals finetune their communication skills to improve their executive presence and effectiveness in the workplace. Her many years of singing on the professional stage helped her hone the art of influence and impactful communication.

A sought-after public speaker, Caroline presents to global audiences, and her TEDxWomen talk about reframing failure and defining success on your own terms has been celebrated as a must-watch resource. Caroline hosts the three-time award-winning podcast, *Your Working Life,* available on all major podcast platforms. She is a contributor to Ellevate Network and LinkedIn. Her video series about career and life empowerment is available on YouTube. Her first book, *This Is Not the Career I Ordered: Empowering Strategies from Women Who Recharged, Reignited, and Reinvented Their Careers,* is still inspiring readers and has been translated into Chinese.

Find out more about Caroline by visiting her website at CarolineDowdHiggins.com.

WORK WITH CAROLINE

Caroline Dowd-Higgins is a sought-after public speaker, bestselling author, certified executive coach, and international media personality. Her books, podcasts, videos, and blogs are enjoyed around the world.

A celebrated keynoter and National Speakers Association member, Caroline speaks at in-person and virtual events with audiences ranging from 50 to 5,000 on how to increase professional influence, magnify impact, and create a culture that honors workplace well-being to empower individuals to thrive. From the boardroom to the training room to the convention hall, she connects with her audience in a way that leaves each person feeling as if they are the only one in the room.

Her North Star is helping people and organizations make a positive impact by discovering and developing their leadership strengths. You can engage with Caroline in a variety of different ways.

Individual Executive Leadership Coaching – From mid-career professionals to new C-suite executive leaders, Caroline helps clients navigate their unique journey to overcome challenges, hone signature strengths, and mitigate blind spots to perform as an impact player. From building a deep leadership bench for company succession planning to retaining top talent, executive coaching empowers individuals to expand self-awareness, discover solutions, and make and implement better decisions.

Mastermind Communities Group Leader – Navigate and accelerate your journey with other industry leaders in a virtual space with psychological safety to explore vulnerabilities, challenges, and opportunities. Curated, small groups of leaders allow you to shift awareness into action and clarify your goals and shared experiences in a supportive setting designed for peer-leader learning and connection.

Extraordinary Team Development – Teamwork is essential for a successful workplace. Caroline helps teams communicate better, improves developmental feedback, and takes a holistic view of a team's strengths and blind spots to develop and achieve transformative goals. Designing a healthy and productive workplace culture is a team effort, and Caroline helps organizations navigate the new opportunities of hybrid, in-person, and remote work to create inclusive and future-focused teams.

Dynamic Keynote Presenter and Workshop Facilitator – With firsthand industry experience, Caroline delivers compelling and motivational presentations and interactive training sessions to empower the modern careerist with practical and implementable action steps, so they can overcome obstacles and prosper. No stranger to the stage, Caroline is entertaining, educational, and compelling and leaves her audiences wanting more.

Find out more about Caroline by visiting her website at CarolineDowdHiggins.com.

YOUR WORKING
LIFE PODCAST

Your Working Life is a three-time award-winning podcast series hosted by career and professional development author, speaker, and influencer, Caroline Dowd-Higgins. Featuring candid interviews with luminaries in the career, leadership, entrepreneurship, and wellness fields, listeners benefit from wisdom about how to navigate life and career. Well-known personalities and industry experts, including **Tiffany Cross, Whitney Johnson, Melissa Daimler, Guy Kawasaki,** and **Marcus Buckingham,** share their personal takes on how to thrive in your life and career. The podcast features a diverse array of experts with a special emphasis on female leaders, authors, and entrepreneurs.

Caroline has interviewed over 500 business leaders, authors, and subject matter experts. The broadcast reach is over one million, with listeners in the USA and 16 countries around the world.

Your Working Life is available on all major podcast listening platforms.

ENDNOTES

1 Whitney Johnson, *Smart Growth: How to Grow Your People to Grow Your Company*, (Boston, Harvard Business Review Press, 2022).

2 Mary Abbajay, *Managing Up: How to Move Up, Win at Work, and Succeed with Any Type of Boss*, (Hoboken, NJ, Wiley, 2018).

3 Caroline Dowd-Higgins (TEDXWomen, *Reinventing a Career and Defining Success on Your Own Terms*) 2020.

4 Howard Thurman, *The Living Wisdom of Howard Thurman: A Visionary for Our Time* (Sounds True Audio, 2010).

5 Marcus Buckingham, *Love and Work: How to Find What You Love, Love What You Do, and Do It for the Rest of Your Life* (Boston, Harvard Business Review Press) 2022.

6 Liz Wiseman, *Multipliers: How the Best Leaders Make Everyone Smarter*, (New York: Harper Business, 2010).

7 Liz Wiseman, *Multipliers: How the Best Leaders Make Everyone Smarter*, (New York: Harper Business, 2010).

8 Brené Brown, (TED, *The Power of Vulnerability*) 2012.

9 Resting Bitch Face. (2022, October 22). In *Wikipedia*. https://en.wikipedia.org/wiki/Resting_bitch_face.

10 Leidy Klotz, *Subtract: The Untapped Science of Less*, (New York, Flat Iron Books, 2021).

11 Brené Brown, *Dare to Lead*, (New York, Penguin Random House, 2018).

12 Merriam-Webster, "Perfection," *Merriam-Webster*, accessed November 12, 2022, https://www.merriam-webster.com/dictionary/perfection.

13 Reshma Saujani, *Brave, Not Perfect* (New York, Currency, 2019).

14 Reshma Saujani, (TED, *Teach Girls Bravery, Not Perfection*) 2016.

15 Kim Scott, *Radical Candor: Be a Kick-Ass Boss Without Losing Your Humanity*, (New York, St. Martin's Press, 2019).

16 Linda Kaplan Thaler and Robin Koval, *Grit to Great: How Perseverance, Passion, and Pluck Take You From Ordinary to Extraordinary* (New York, Crown Business, 2015).

17 American Psychological Association, "Work and Well-being Survey Reports, 2022" https://www.apa.org/pubs/reports/work-well-being.

18 Arianna Huffington, *The Sleep Revolution: Transforming Your Life, One Night at a Time*, (New York, Harmony Books, 2016).

19 Adam Grant, PhD (TED, *How to Stop Languishing and Start Finding Flow*) 2021.

20 Jason Lippert, president and CEO, LCI Industries, https://www.lci1.com/culture/.

21 Paula Davis, *Beating Burnout at Work: Why Teams Hold the Secret to Well-Being & Resilience*, (Philadelphia: Wharton School Press, 2021).

22 Paula Davis, "You Can't Yoga Your Way Out of Burnout," *Forbes*, March 2, 2021.

23 World Health Organization, "Burn-out an 'occupational phenomenon': International Classification of Diseases," May 28, 2019, https://www.who.int/news/item/28-05-2019-burn-out-an-occupational-phenomenon-international-classification-of-diseases.

24 Christina Maslach, PhD., Professor of Psychology Emerita, core researcher- Healthy Workplaces Center, University of California, Berkeley https://psychology.berkeley.edu/people/christina-maslach.

25 Saundra Dalton-Smith, M.D., *Sacred Rest: Recover Your Life, Renew Your Energy, Restore Your Sanity* (New York, Nashville: FaithWords, 2017).

26 Melissa Daimler, *ReCulturing: Design Your Company Culture to Connect with Strategy and Purpose for Lasting Success,* (New York: McGraw Hill, 2022).

27 Katie Taylor, "What does psychological safety mean, anyway?" Atlassian Teamwork, February 18, 2022, https://www.atlassian.com/blog/teamwork/what-does-psychological-safety-mean-anyway.

28 Amy C. Edmonson (TED, *How to Turn a Group of Strangers into a Team*) 2017.

29 Joe Sanok, *Thursday is the New Friday, How to Work Fewer Hours, Make More Money, and Spent Tine Doing What You Want,* (USA: Harper Collins Leadership, 2021).

30 Juliet Funt, *A Minute to Think: Reclaim Creativity, Conquer Busyness, and Do Your Best Work,* (USA: Harper Business, 2021).

31 Sarah Goff-Dupont, "10 teamwork tips custom built for 2022," Atlassian Teamwork, February 17, 2022, https://www.atlassian.com/blog/teamwork/teamwork-tips-for-2022.

32 Devora Zack, *Singletasking: Get More Done—One Thing at a Time,* (Oakland, CA: Berrett Koehler Publishers, 2015).

33 Diane Sieg, Founder – The Resilience Academy https://dianesieg.com

34 Jim Collins, *Built to Last: Successful Habits of Visionary Companies,* (New York, Harper Collins, 2002).

35 Kat Boogard, "Hear us out! If you're not doing these 3 things, you're not practicing active listening," Atlassian Leadership, March 4, 2022, https://www.atlassian.com/blog/leadership/active-listening-3-things.

36 Charlotte Beers, *I'd Rather Be in Charge: A Legendary Business Leader's Roadmap for Achieving Pride, Power, and Joy at Work*, (New York, Vanguard Press, 2012).

37 John Klessinger, *A Coach's Manual: Everything You Need to Know to Be a Successful Coach* (Maryland, Championship Productions) 2021.

38 Brian Elliott, Sheela Subramanian, and Helen Kupp, *How the Future Works: Leading Flexible Teams to Do the Best Work of Their Lives* (Hoboken, NJ, Wiley) 2022.

39 Future Forum, https://futureforum.com/about/.